PARENTING
THE
WILD CHILD

BOOKS BY MILES McPHERSON

21 Jump-Start Devotional

Bad to the Bone

Parenting the Wild Child

The Power of Believing in Your Child

Miles McPherson

PARENTING
THE
WILD CHILD

BETHANY HOUSE PUBLISHERS
MINNEAPOLIS, MINNESOTA 55438

Published by Bethany House Publishers
A Ministry of Bethany Fellowship International
11400 Hampshire Avenue South
Minneapolis, Minnesota 55438
www.bethanyhouse.com

Printed in the United States of America by
Bethany Press International, Minneapolis, Minnesota 55438

Library of Congress Cataloging-in-Publication Data

McPherson, Miles.
   Parenting the wild child : hope for those with an out of control teenager / by Miles McPherson.
       p.   cm.
     ISBN 0-7642-2370-4
     1. Parent and teenager—United States.   2. Problem children—United States.
3. Parenting—Religious aspects.   I. Title.
HQ799.15 .M39   2000
649'.153—dc21
                                                          00-009925

To the parents who feel lost

in their attempt to deliver

their kids from

"wild child" status.

Too often I have looked into the hopeless eyes of parents who have tried everything they could think of in order to save the lives of their children. Most of the time, I have felt helpless. Consequently, I prayerfully designed this book to be a tool for them in their battle. My hope and prayer is that it will help save lives.

MILES McPHERSON is president and founder of Miles Ahead Ministries and speaks to hundreds of thousands of teens and adults each year. A former defensive back with the San Diego Chargers, Miles is a nationally known evangelist and the founder of The Rock Church, which meets at San Diego University. Miles and his wife make their home in San Diego with their three children.

In his ministry Miles has talked to young people from all walks of life—one-on-one and in youth rallies of thousands. He knows what makes them tick, especially rebellious teenagers. That's because he was one. As a junior in high school, Miles started smoking marijuana, which led to cocaine use as a rookie in the NFL. In 1984, however, he committed his life to the Lord. From that point on, he was delivered from his drug habit, stopped using foul language, and was reunited with his girlfriend, Debbie, who is now his wife. After earning a Master of Divinity from Azusa Pacific University, Miles began his ministry and is now a featured speaker at some of the nation's largest youth and adult events. His Miles Ahead Crusades, which target unsaved teenagers, have been used to bring over 23,000 young people to Christ since 1996.

Miles can be seen live on the Internet Sunday evenings at www.milesahead.com.

Contents

Introduction

TRAVELING AROUND THE COUNTRY and talking to and about kids has many great benefits. I have had the privilege of meeting countless young people who are sold out for the Lord. I cannot tell you how encouraging it is to meet young people who have begun ministries on their campuses, led their parents to the Lord, and overcome incredible challenges in their lives. But the other side of the story is meeting families who are in pain because their child is out of control. He or she is the "wild child" of the bunch.

Some of these kids represent a parent's worse nightmare: the sexually active teenage daughter, the sixteen-year-old son who joins a gang, the child who runs away time after time, the drug-addicted son. Parents approach me at church or at crusades and plead, "My son is on drugs and won't stay home. What do I do?" "I think my daughter is sleeping around. What do I do?"

"My son won't listen to a thing I say. What do I do?"

For so long I have felt inadequate to answer these questions. It can take a lot of work to sort out the issues, and even when I had a possible solution, it often required a lengthy explanation. Now I can finally empower those parents and you with *Parenting the Wild Child*.

Because there are countless ways a young person can be a wild child, it would require thousands of pages to cover solutions to all of those problems. However, I have come to realize that wild children are going through an unseen spiritual battle. And in this book I address the universal principles necessary to set your family free and to fight this battle from a position of strength instead of weakness. I also present many practical suggestions for parenting a difficult teenager. Although some of these suggestions may not apply to your particular situation, the timeless spiritual insights apply to all rebellious children. They will also help you to deal with the conflict in your own soul. Parents often suffer more than their rebellious son or daughter does. Becoming a wiser and stronger parent will help you to better respond to rebellious behavior.

The spiritual battle that the wild child goes through is similar to the physical battle that people experience when destructive cancer cells take over a normally healthy body. In the case of the wild child, he or she is suffering from a spiritual cancer. The cancer (rebelliousness) of the wild child is based on lies and deception. Satan is using his false promises and threats to deceive young people. Once these lies are believed and trusted, they produce grave consequences, which you see played out in the life of the wild child.

As an example of Satan's power, allow me to ask you a question. Have you ever wondered why every time something apparently bad happens, we first react negatively? The Bible clearly says, "My brethren, count it all joy when you fall into various trials, knowing that the testing of your faith produces patience. But let patience have its perfect work, that you may be perfect and complete, lacking nothing" (James 1:2–4).

If Scripture tells us to be joyful in hard times, why do we react the opposite way? I will tell you: Satan whispers it into our ears. He tells us to doubt our abilities, or to feel sorry for ourselves, or to think God has abandoned us, or . . . Not only can Satan lie to us in a particular situation, he keeps on telling us the same five to ten lies, and we believe him. We fall for the same trick every day. We repeat the same mistakes. Through his lies, Satan is convincing all of us, especially young people, to do and think unimaginable things.

The good news is that we, as believers in Jesus, have access to the one thing that can undo the effects of these lies: prayer based on God's truth. If Satan can destroy a life based on a lie, how much more can God repair a life and restore what the locusts have eaten.

Throughout this book I expose thirty-five lies that Satan may be using against you and six he is probably using against your child. More importantly, I present biblical truths, which, if applied properly through prayer, can undo the effects of Satan's lies and bring your child out of his or her rebellion. In addition, at the end of each chapter I outline prayers designed to expose the untruths of these lies and empower you with biblical mandates concerning your responsibilities and privileges as a parent. Each chapter also contains a few review questions to help you think through the issues discussed in the chapter, so you can begin to resolve them in your heart. This will enable you to pray with more focus and take efficient and effective action to help your child.

As you read, you'll see that I emphasize two things: (1) Satan is the enemy and his lies are his number one weapon against your family, and (2) God is your ally and prayer is your most powerful and faithful weapon.

Chapter One

THE WILD CHILD: A CANCER KID

CAROLINE WAS NURSING HER fourth child, Lucy, when she noticed a lump in her breast. She figured it was simply a clogged duct but decided to call a nurse for advice. The nurse agreed that it was probably nothing to worry about; it would probably clear up. And since Caroline already had a doctor's appointment scheduled two weeks later, she decided that if it didn't disappear, it could be checked then.

When Caroline's doctor examined the lump, he immediately ordered further tests. Caroline called her husband, Brad, in tears. A mammogram had revealed a five-centimeter lump. A biopsy confirmed it was malignant. A cancer specialist was immediately sought, and one week later Caroline was in surgery having the lump removed.

When Caroline woke up, she sensed something was wrong. The doctor seemed to be avoiding her. When she confronted him, he told her the cancer had spread to her lymph system.

An extremely difficult road of treatment lay ahead. But Caroline and her family were willing to try anything to save her life. They spent hours meeting with doctors, not only laying out a treatment plan but also implementing it and monitoring its progress. The goal was simple: save Caroline's life. They were committed to securing the best care possible. With four daughters, a husband, and countless friends and relatives who loved her, she had lots to live for.

Each and every one of us is susceptible to cancer. That's because we all have the gene that can trigger cancer.

Genes tell cells what to do, when to do it, and how to do it. All of us have a class of genes known as proto-oncogenes. At some point during the life of a cell, however, these normal genes may become damaged and program cells to start growing and dividing. A gene that causes unrestricted growth is called an oncogene. Most of the time, these defective genes don't cause cancer. Normally another gene, called a tumor suppressor, will create proteins that stop the uncontrolled growth of the cells. However, in cases where the tumor-suppressing gene is also flawed, cancer develops. Cancerous cells have a mind of their own. They take over healthy areas of the body, preventing them from working properly.

So what does cancer have to do with parenting a wild child? Just like cancer causes cells to grow uncontrolled, your child's flesh, in a spiritual sense, is out of control. When young people display rebellious, wild-child behavior, it is a symptom of a spiritual cancer. In most cases, the basic root of their problem is spiritual, not so much emotional, behavioral, or mental. A wild child's flesh is at war with his or her spirit. Galatians 5: 16–21 says:

Walk in the Spirit, and you shall not fulfill the lust of the flesh. For the flesh lusts against the Spirit, and the Spirit against the flesh; and these are contrary to one another, so that you do not do the things that you wish. But if you are led by the Spirit, you are not under the law. Now the works of the flesh are evident, which are: adultery, fornication, uncleanness, lewdness, idolatry, sorcery, hatred, contentions, jealousies, outbursts of wrath, selfish ambitions, dissensions, heresies, envy, murders, drunkenness, revelries, and the like; of which I tell you beforehand, just as I also told you in time past, that those who practice such things will not inherit the kingdom of God.

So when it comes to the wild child, a helpful way of understanding this concept is to view the sinful works of his flesh as the result of mutated proto-oncogenes. Again, each of us has proto-oncogenes, so we all have the potential for developing cancer. In the same way, every child is capable of being overcome by sinful thoughts, feelings, and actions. Their natural tendency to do wrong is at war with God's desire for them to do right. "For the flesh lusts against the Spirit, and the Spirit against the flesh; and these are contrary to one another, so that you do not do the things that you wish" (Galatians 5:17).

From now on you must accept that the wild child is in a spiritual battle. His or her behavior is not a matter of disobeying *our* rules. They are disobeying *God's* law because they are losing the spiritual battle. In no way does this excuse children from being responsible for their actions, but it will affect how you view and approach the problem.

As I said earlier, one of the most mysterious aspects of cancer is that everyone has proto-oncogenes in their body; therefore, everyone has the ability to develop cancer. It is only when something causes the proto-oncogene to be mutated that you actually contract the disease itself. Unfortunately, why this happens in some people and not in others is not completely understood.

The flesh of every child (and adult, for that matter) has the potential to grow out of control, thus taking over his normal, or godly, purpose and function. Whether we want to accept it or not, we all could become drunkards, liars, murderers, fornicators, or adulterers. It is very dangerous to think that we are above these temptations. As 1 Corinthians 10:12 says, "Therefore let him who thinks he stands take heed lest he fall."

With rebellion, there's no mystery as to what—or who—is behind the spiritual oppression that causes spiritual cancer. Satan has invaded the life of your child, mutating and feeding his flesh with selfish desires and creating opportunities that will lead to nothing but death.

LIE #1: The wild child is the enemy.

Satan is the Father of Lies and a murderer. And he has one goal in mind: to steal your child by lying to him about his life's purpose and true source of happiness.

Satan has victimized young people in ways that words cannot explain. The spiritual battle that our children are under is beyond the understanding and ability of mere humans to conquer. Children's minds and hearts are being assaulted in the spiritual realm in an attempt by Satan to misdirect their paths for living. It is very important for you, the parent, to comprehend the battle that the wild child is in. Once understood, a game plan and appropriate weapons can be chosen to help your child win this battle, but understanding and wisdom are the keys.

You must agree that Satan, not your child, is the enemy.

And Satan's number one weapon is his ability to lie. John 8:44 says Satan is the Father of Lies. In fact, the truth is not in him. That means Satan might tell you that your wild child is the enemy. But that's a lie. Satan is the real enemy, and lies are his weapon. God is your only hope; and prayer based on the truth of His Word is your number one weapon. Let me say that again: God is your ally and prayer is the most powerful weapon available.

Throughout this book I will emphasize the power of prayer in battling the trials and challenges of the wild child. You will learn how to pray and what to pray for in each situation you might face. No matter what your wild child is struggling with—drugs, sex, witchcraft, gangs, stealing, you name it— these are only symptoms of Satan's spiritual bondage. Therefore, in the end, the highest and most complete solution to the wild child's problems is to be set free spiritually.

The only biblical goal you should desire for your child is godliness. If a child is truly walking with God and the Holy Spirit is guiding his or her life, sinful ways are going to change: "If anyone is in Christ, he is a new creation; old things have passed away; behold, all things have become new" (2 Corinthians 5:17).

When a wild child reaches out to God, his destructive attitudes and desires will be transformed. His life will change. As a parent, this must be the focus of your prayers. Most parents fall into the trap of desiring a change in behavior, but that solution is short of God's goal. If the wild child's heart is not renewed, a behavior change will only last for a time. In addition, the new behavior may not be any better than the original problem.

Proverbs 4:23 says, "Keep your heart with all diligence, for out of it spring the issues of life." Did you catch that? The heart is the source of not only godly attitudes and actions but also evil, such as murder, cursing, and the like. That is why God desires a clean heart in us. So if you want your child to change, pray for his heart. God wants to cleanse your child of his sinful nature and transform him into something that will glorify Him. First John 1:9 tells us that two things happen when we repent. First, we are forgiven; but second, we are cleansed from un-righteousness. This means that the wild child's desires will be cleansed away and replaced with a hunger and thirst for right-eousness. And once a heart is cleansed, a life can be trans-formed.

Many parents think their wild child is a lost cause, but nothing is lost or impossible with God. Have realistic expecta-tions, but also have *Himpossible* prayer requests.

Every miracle in the Bible is a testimony to the fact that Jesus changes lives. When He healed a paralytic in Capernaum, witnesses said, "We never saw anything like this!" (Mark 2:12). The change you desire in your child requires a miracle; there-fore, you need to begin asking for and expecting the miracle of your child falling in love with God.

LIE #2: You have the right to demand a child to stop his or her wildness before you understand the wildness.

Your number one goal is to begin developing a ministry to your child, one through which Jesus can transform his life.

This cannot be illustrated more vividly than Jesus' encoun-ter with the woman at the well (John 4:1–26). As you may re-call, Jesus was sitting by a well when a woman from Samaria approached. He asked her for a drink. Now, in those days Jews and the Samaritans did not associate. In addition, public con-versations were prohibited between men and women who were strangers. But Jesus broke all the man-made rules. He knew the woman had had five husbands. He knew that she needed the water of everlasting life, which only He could give. So instead of doing what was politically correct, instead of brushing her off as a harlot, he ministered to her according to her need. He knew and addressed her need in such a way that she could receive from Him and be blessed. Jesus' number one concern was for her salvation and freedom from her pain.

Your wild child is in pain. He has an intense need for God in his life. Yes, when he acts out his behavior is wrong and must be dealt with, but inside that body is a hurting boy. You do not need to coddle or make things easy for him, but he needs your help. Are you prepared to provide it?

It can be hard for parents to change how they approach the wild child. For many, the relationship has become a battle. Most communication is in the form of arguments or attempts to discipline. To help convert your attitude toward treatment of this cancer from one based on the law to one based on grace, try to understand your child's actions. What are the reasons behind the madness in his life?

As you'll learn later in the book, discipline is still needed in parenting. For now, though, it is important to pray about how God wants you to discipline your child. Remember, there is a spiritual component to his behavior. What spiritual lessons can be taught through how you discipline? Another way of thinking about it is: How you react to your child's behavior can impact how he views God and his relationship with God.

Understanding Adolescence

When I was young, my father was very faithful in taking our family on trips to the mountains. Often my uncle would join us and take us hunting, fishing, and camping. We'd pack the car at five in the morning and head off to the mountains no matter what the weather was—snow, rain, or sunshine. One day they planned a ski trip for both of our families. With two cars and ten kids, we got a late start and drove two hours before stopping for dinner and checking into a local hotel. The next morning a heavy snowstorm hit the area. It was extremely difficult to see where we were going, but we were determined to find the ski resort and hit the slopes. We drove up into the mountains and through valleys and several towns looking for a ski slope through the snow. We literally spent the day in the car. Finally, my dad decided to give up and return to the hotel. As we approached it, we saw something very interesting—there was a ski slope right across the highway. The whole time we had tried our best to find our destination, but the snow, the confusion of ten kids, and never having been in the area before made finding our way very difficult. This experience is very similar to what teenagers go through.

Your child is trying hard to find his way through adolescence. He is trying to figure out who he is, but a snowstorm is falling all around him, clouding his way.

Of course, every child is different, but most teenagers change direction a lot. You'll see it in their behavior or notice how they change their minds frequently. They seem to do things in opposites almost daily. One moment they'll dress a certain way, listen to a particular type of music, or hang out with a certain group of friends. The next moment all that has changed.

An adolescent is trying to separate himself from his young, childlike self so that he can become a young adult. This sometimes means separating himself from you, the parent. He is likely trying to figure out which version of himself "fits" the world. What kind of life does he want to develop and pursue? You may notice that he doesn't like being around you in public, and wants to show you less and less affection. More than any-thing, this is just a sign that he is growing into adulthood.

Your job and responsibility is to help your child through adolescence. But the million-dollar question is, "How?" Many parents are clueless about what their kids need in order to become young adults. Yes, there are certain things we don't want our kids to do and other things we wish they were doing. But some parents overreact to the poor choices their teenagers make. They lose sight of the big picture. An instance of relatively minor misbehavior has less long-term effect on a child than his learning to be an independent, mature adult.

I have heard countless complaints about kids and their behavior. Sometimes I am shocked beyond belief, not always at what the child is doing but at what the parents think is bad. Once I was called into a meeting with a mom who was desperate to talk to someone about her son. She was in a panic and extremely worried about her Jimmy. I got the impression that the boy was one step away from the juvenile detention center. Once we sat down and sorted everything out, I learned that she was upset because her son was not going to church. Yes, church is important. But in this case, it was not a sign of out-and-out rebellion.

At the same time, what makes parenting such a tough job is that it's a mistake to think a wild child's behavior is not that serious. Every once in a while, I hear someone say, "My child is just going through a phase. She'll grow out of it." There is no such thing as harmless, rebellious behavior. Again, not every sign of rebellion is the end of the world, but it must be dealt with immediately. You can't ignore it for six months, six weeks, or even six days. The sooner you acknowledge problems and begin to at least pray about solutions and remedies, the better. This will not only prevent you from allowing things to get out of hand but will also help develop a habit of being proactive when it comes to your children. They will soon figure out that Mom and Dad are on the job, that you don't miss anything.

It's important to pray for discernment about what your child is rebelling against. Has some family situation caused it? She may be responding to family dysfunction. Acknowledging this possibility in your family takes courage. To help identify a pattern of dysfunction, think back to how it was in your family growing up. If there was some sort of dysfunction in your childhood, there is a good chance it now exists in your family to some degree. If this is so, it would be wise to seek outside help, which I will discuss later in this chapter.

Whatever the reason for the wild child's behavior, you must ask yourself, "Is it an outward expression of an inward battle?"

What Is Wild?

Every child and family is different, so it's up to you to decide what constitutes rebellion for your child. It may be necessary to assess the situation and decide what battles you are going to fight first. If your child runs away, takes drugs, and is having sex, you are right. He is rebellious.

The first thing to do is to list the things you believe are making your child a wild child. Again, this will be different from family to family.

- Does he talk back?
- Is he sexually active?
- Is he rude to you and/or your spouse?
- Does he run away?
- Does he live with someone else and won't communicate with you?
- Is he involved in a cult?

- Is he suicidal?
- Is he addicted to drugs? alcohol? something else?
- Is he in a gang?
- Is he in jail? Does he have criminals for friends?

Come up with your own list, and whether it's short or long, start prioritizing the problems. Are one or two more critical than the others? Are any the cause of other problems? It is important for you to clearly identify and write down the problems. This list will be invaluable as you learn how God can help your wild child and your family. Also, Satan is the master of deception and illusion, and you might discover that he has made things appear worse than they really are.

LIE #3: The wild child has no reason for his or her wildness.

Destructive behavior is the symptom of some kind of pain that Satan is exploiting. The wild child acts the way he does because there is something very unsettled in his life and heart. Bad behavior does not come from nowhere. There is always a reason that a child acts out in a way we call *wild*. Even if your teen has been rebelling or living a destructive lifestyle, it is still true that he is searching for something. Discovering what this is and beginning to minister to this need are at the center of your ministry to your child. As you think about his actions, there are several questions to answer:

1. How does he rebel or act wild?
2. Is he predominantly inflicting pain on himself or lashing out at others?
3. Is there a pattern to his behavior?

(a) Does he act out only at night? during the day? or does it vary?

(b) Does something frequently happen before he acts out? (an argument at home? another child receives praise? was he talking to a certain person or about a certain subject?)

(c) Did the behavior begin when you moved to another school or neighborhood?

(d) Can you tell what he's thinking when he acts out?

Sometimes the reason for rebellion is obvious. Johnny was basically a normal, emotionally healthy child. He and his dad did things together on a regular basis. He got along with the other kids on the block. But then his dad died, and Johnny changed overnight. He became a loner and wasn't interested in the things he used to do. He became angry at the world. It was obvious that losing his dad had a profound effect on him.

Other reasons for rebellion are not so easy to pinpoint. Some childhood problems are never discovered. People never figure out what went wrong with a kid, but it is still important to do the best we can to provide help.

The next thing you must consider is what does a "nonwild" child look like?

I have often spoken with parents who complain and complain about their child, but when I ask what they want their child to do, they say something like, "I want him to act right." Well, what does that mean? What are your expectations? What does "nonwild" look like? For example, is it not talking back? Is there a certain attitude that needs to change? Do you want him to stop drinking? Stop having sex? Or are there positive things you want him to begin doing?

Once you assess the problem, test yourselves to see if you and your spouse agree on how serious the problems are. On a scale of 1 to 10, ask each other how bad you think the problem is. One way to decide this is to think about how bad it would get if the wildness went totally unchecked for a month, six months, or a year. If both of you do not have the same urgency about the problem, you won't have the same resolve for getting it solved. If there is a difference of opinion, you must discuss why this is true. This will help both of you get on the same page as it pertains to your treatment schedule.

Next, what is your motivation for wanting to change your child's behavior? To save face? To show off your "good" kid or to avoid being embarrassed? If your main goal is not to help your wild child become a productive, godly adult, as his parents you will not achieve God's purpose, and you will fail in the discipline of your child.

It is also important for parents or guardians to agree on the goals and the process of the battle. A house divided cannot stand. This journey will undoubtedly bring stress into your home and relationships, and this, too, is part of Satan's strategy. Both parents must realize there isn't a "quick fix" to the problem. A disciplined, planned strategy is essential.

Once you have identified the spiritual cancer that is attacking your child and have begun to think about a plan for treatment, it will also help you to divide and conquer. Identify the source or sources of the spiritual cancer. When I say "source," I mean where the cancer originated and from where it continues to draw strength. For example, perhaps your child's spiritual cancer is being fed by his friends, music, TV, or the Internet. Second, once these sources are identified, begin to administer treatment for each source. And don't forget to treat the actual disease. Know its risks. A parent should not try to fight a child's drug abuse problem without knowing the effects of the particular drug or drugs. This information will be very helpful when talking with the child about his spiritual cancer. The same would be true for a teenager who is sexually active. Let her know the risks and consequences of her behavior.

Your child will probably not change overnight. It is going to be a process, and the timetable is totally up to God. This is not something you will deal with in one swoop. You will best deal with it one bite at a time.

Hope deferred makes the heart sick. In other words, when you are expecting something and don't get it, you're bound to be hurt or disappointed. One way to prevent this is to accept the fact that improvement will likely occur gradually. Make a commitment to stick it out, but define what this means. Until he turns eighteen? I hope it's longer than that. When you got married, you took a vow that went something like this: "For richer or for poorer, in sickness and in health, for better or for worse, until death do us part."

Well, that vow also applies to our kids, for the most part. They will eventually leave our home and move on in life, but they will still be our kids, and we must be willing to stick with them.

Barry grew up in the home of successful parents who could give him anything he wanted. But at the age of only thirteen he began using heroin. For years he used heroin and drank alcohol. He was eventually put into prison, where he was beaten up several times. This tormented his parents, but they never gave up, and they methodically dealt with his problems one at a time. Undoubtedly, looking back, they would admit to making mistakes; but in the end the one thing that got them through was a commitment to stick it out until the end. No matter how bad things got, they loved and supported their son.

They were determined not to allow Satan to defeat them and destroy their family.

First, accept the fact that things will get worse before they get better, and prepare yourself for this. This will help you to overcome the first wave of disappointment that Satan will try to destroy you with. Second, evaluate your family priorities. How far you are willing to go? This can be a dangerous question. The reality is that focusing so much on a wild child may cause you and your family to suffer even more. Strive for a healthy balance. "Nonwild" children tend to be forgotten or overlooked in situations like this. Don't ignore them and simply believe they will be okay. This is a perfect time to build on the positives in their lives and behavior. Identify the strengths of their character, praise their willingness to play by the rules, and encourage their commitment to God. This will act as cement as you attempt to keep them on the right path.

LIE #4: You have a right not to allow the problems of your wild child to interfere with your life.

Don't ever say, "I am not going to let my child's problems interfere with my life. I am not going to allow his mistakes to ruin my personal plans." Don't get me wrong. You should not let your child's problems absolutely ruin your life. But I have seen too many parents suffer more than they needed to.

In the end, teenagers are responsible for their troubles and behavior, but until they reach adulthood, your child *should* be your life. Our children are our heritage from the Lord. They are who we point to as evidence that we were faithful in living for the Lord. This does not mean that if they turn out "bad" we did something wrong, but it does mean that if we believe Satan's lies and give up trying to raise our children, we are worse than an infidel: "But if anyone does not provide for his own, and especially for those of his household, he has denied the faith and is worse than an unbeliever" (1 Timothy 5:8).

Not only do we have God-given responsibilities toward our children, the longer we ignore the seriousness of child rebellion, the more difficult it will be to deal with it. In addition, as Moses warns in Numbers 32:23, "Then take note, you have sinned against the Lord; and be sure your sin will find you out." Because your child is your responsibility, the sin of ignoring the problem will not only find you out but it will also consume your life more than you could ever imagine. There is NO WAY you can ignore it indefinitely. Your child's issues will find you out.

Decide to be on the offense rather than the defense. Overwhelm the problem with prayer, counsel, and activity before it overwhelms you with stress, fear, and hopelessness. But there does come a time when you are sacrificing the whole for the part. This line can be drawn in the form of time, behavior, money, or stress on your relationship. As time passes, you will be able to more intelligently assess the problem and progress in your ability to deal with it. Making initial deadlines and measurements will help you mark your progress and avoid the feeling that there is no end in sight.

You must be very careful to balance the feelings you will experience as they pertain to your child. One day she will be the enemy: stealing from you, cursing at you, and out to ruin your life. The next day she'll be your beloved child again. This roller coaster of emotions can be overwhelming if you are not prepared to deal with it properly. It will be at these times of confusion and despair that you must remember the battle and the real enemy: Satan. You must strive to give your child the best opportunity to live a normal life. One of the ways to deal with the seesaw of emotions is to make a covenant to renew your commitment to your goals each night before you go to bed. "Be angry, and do not sin. Do not let the sun go down on your wrath" (Ephesians 4:26).

This verse tells us two things that are helpful in this situation. Obviously, you should not let the sun go down on your anger. Remember that there is room to be angry and mad, but no room to sin and to become a rebellious parent. You cannot rebel against God's mandate and privilege of being a parent with the responsibility of doing your best to raise your child. In other words, you must not let any anger or frustration throw you off course as you implement His plan for your child. Therefore, before you go to sleep, remember to add a prayer for your wild child: *Dear Lord, thank you for my son/daughter _____. I praise you for giving me/us this opportunity to raise him/her.*

Be committed to finding a specialist to help your family. It is okay, and not a sign of weakness. When Caroline's lump on her breast was discovered, not for one second did she think that she could fix it herself. Her family immediately sought professional help.

This book provides a lot of guidance, but with so many possible wild-child situations, it will also lead to many questions. There are people who have been trained to answer the questions this book will raise in your life.

Proverbs 24:6 says, "For by wise counsel you will wage your own war, and in a multitude of counselors there is safety." And in Luke 14:31 we're asked, "Or what king, going to make war against another king, does not sit down first and consider whether he is able with ten thousand to meet him who comes against him with twenty thousand?" You are in a war that you cannot win alone. This counsel will help you to make a true assessment of the nature and seriousness of your child's spiritual cancer.

Your situation is more complicated and complex than you know. The battle you are in is not between you and your child. No! It is between your family and the devil. He is manipulating your child. Again, this does not mean your child is not responsible for his actions, but he is not your enemy. He is not sitting up at night thinking of ways to destroy your life. A specialist will help you work through the many issues you are facing. But whom do you go to?

When I have to get my teeth worked on, I go to a professional dentist. When I need my car worked on, I go to a trained mechanic to fix it. If you get to the point that you do not completely understand what is making your child wild, it is time to get an outside opinion.

You deserve and need the best help available for the problem you are facing. This is why it is vitally important to talk with a number of people. The Bible says there is safety in a multitude of counsel (Proverbs 11:14). Discuss your situation with the youth pastor at your church or the parents of other wild children. And just because there is a spiritual component to parenting a wild child, it does not mean a pastor is always the best person to provide help. Satan has access to all areas of our lives, and if he has tormented your child in deep emotional issues, a professional counselor trained in children's emotional issues could be your best alternative.

As I conclude this chapter, allow me to contradict myself. Even though this battle is more complicated than you realize, you will at times be the only one able to figure out what is going on. In other words, your child is *your* child. Become a student of your child's problem. If you pay close attention, you will be able to monitor your child's progress like no one else can. You have known him or her since birth, and with the right counsel and insight, you will be able to reverse some of the conditions that have caused the problem. At times you will be the only one to hear God on specific issues facing your family. Remember, the only biblical goal you should desire for your child is godliness. If a child is truly walking with God and the Holy Spirit is guiding his or her life, sinful ways are going to change.

Review Questions
1. What is your definition of wild behavior?
2. What does "nonwild" look like to you?
3. When does your child act out?
4. What do you think is the source of your child's pain?

Chemo-Prayers Time
Lie #1: The wild child is the enemy.
Dear Lord, thank you for your Word. Thank you for exposing Satan for who he really is, the Enemy, the Destroyer, the Evil One, the Accuser. I pray that you would grant me the wisdom to wage this battle in the spiritual realm. I realize that the weapons you have given for this battle are mighty. As 2 Corinthians 10:4 says, "For the weapons of our warfare are not carnal but mighty in God for pulling down strongholds." Lord, may I fight the appropriate enemy with the proper weapons.

Lie #2: You have the right to demand a child to stop his or her wildness before you understand the wildness.
Dear Lord, I realize that Proverbs 18:13 says, "He who answers a matter before he hears it, it is folly and shame to him." Lord, if I am not sure what I am asking my child to change from, it is not likely that I know what I am asking him/her to change

into. May I not be so foolish as to require my child to provide the answer—a changed life—when I am not sure what the real question or problem is.

Lie #3: The wild child has no reason for his or her wildness.

Dear Lord, thank you for your Word. I pray that you would give me compassion for my child's problem and the spiritual battle he/she is losing. I am tired and want to give up. Please grant me discernment that I may understand the true nature of my child's problem. James 1:5–6 says, "If any of you lacks wisdom, let him ask of God, who gives to all liberally and without reproach, and it will be given to him. But let him ask in faith, with no doubting, for he who doubts is like a wave of the sea driven and tossed by the wind." Please grant me wisdom into my wild child's situation.

Lie #4: You have a right not to allow the problems of your wild child to interfere with your life.

Dear Lord, thank you for your Word. I pray that I would realize and understand the awesome privilege you have given me to raise my children. Psalm 127:3 says, "Behold, children are a heritage from the Lord, The fruit of the womb is His reward." I pray that I would receive and handle the responsibility to care for my child with an unselfish and sacrificial attitude. You said in John 15:13, "Greater love has no one than this, than to lay down one's life for his friends." You laid down your life for me. I must certainly be willing to lay down my life for the good of my children.

WILD ACCESS: A ROLLER COASTER RIDE

IF YOU EVER WONDERED why cancer is so hard to cure, here's one big reason: it has a mind of its own. As I mentioned earlier, cancerous cells grow out of control, unsuppressed by the body's natural defenses. Cancer cells multiply faster than normal healthy cells. At times they divide so quickly that they produce condensed batches of cells called tumors that can kill organs and eventually the person with the cancer. But what makes cancer so difficult to cure is the fact that it can seemingly outthink even the doctors who are trained to kill it.

In a way, cancer cells can reprogram healthy cells to act as they do. When God designed our cells, he gave them the ability to eat, breathe, drink, discard waste products, and reproduce. Deep inside its nucleus, the very middle of the cell, is the DNA, where all the decisions are made for the cell. It is the DNA that tells the cell what to become and how to function.

One of the ways cancer can affect healthy cells is to reprogram their DNA, thus changing their function. In other words, a perfectly healthy liver cell that is designed to function as a liver can all of a sudden cease to act as a liver cell. Once enough liver cells cease to act as normal liver cells, the organ dies and it is no longer able to fulfill its function. The body suffers, too, and will ultimately die.

Satan is looking for the same result on a spiritual level. He is fully aware of the potential of your child's mind, heart, and soul, but he needs her to surrender those abilities to him. He will do everything he can to reprogram a child's mind, her desires, her actions. The symptoms of this reprogramming are evident in virtually every newspaper. Think about it: why would a teenage girl have a baby, dump it in a trash can, and return to her prom? Why would a couple of teenage boys carry out a plan to kill the Christian students in their school? Satan is ultimately behind these acts, planting thoughts and justifying motives in the minds of young people. And he's been doing it for a long, long time. When Judas betrayed Jesus, the Bible tells us that Satan was involved: "Then Satan entered Judas, surnamed Iscariot, who was numbered among the twelve" (Luke 22:3).

I am not implying that demon possession is the cause of your child's problems. I am saying that satanic influence is definitely involved.

Satan was also at work in the life of Peter. When Jesus was preparing His disciples for His crucifixion, Peter denied that He should be turned over, beaten, and crucified. Jesus' response tells it all: "But when He had turned around and looked at His disciples, He rebuked Peter, saying, 'Get behind Me, Satan! For you are not mindful of the things of God, but the things of men' " (Mark 8:33). Why else would Jesus tell Satan to back off instead of Peter?

Satan has a way of putting in the minds of our children the things of this dark, evil world. Begin praying that God would renew the mind of your child and that she would begin to meditate on godly things rather than worldly trappings.

Spiritual cancer and physical cancer are alike in other ways besides the reprogramming that takes place. To keep growing, physical cancer can provide its own food supply. When cancer cells are densely grouped, they form a tumor, but sometimes the tumor gets too big for its own good. It no longer gets the nourishment it needs. When this happens, the cancer cells stimulate the body to grow additional capillaries to the area to provide additional nourishment.

In the same way, Satan will feed your child's spiritual cancer. He will help her find the people, places, and things needed to continue her destructive life. Have you ever asked yourself, "Where did my daughter find that guy?" "Where did my son get those drugs?" "Where did my son learn to speak like that?" The answer is Satan. You can blame your child's friends, the neighborhood, or the Internet, but these are only tools in the hands of the devil. He is behind their being supplied to the wild child. He will create new sources of trouble in order to stay in business. Remember, cancer has no intention of going away on its own. It will continue to fight and fight for more control until the patient is dead.

Spiritual cancer and physical cancer are also similar in their defense mechanisms. When chemotherapy is used to fight cancer, a chemical is injected in the veins. This chemical is absorbed into the cancer cells (as well as the healthy cells). It starts to kill them by destroying the DNA. Before the next round of chemotherapy, however, the cancer cells can do an amazing thing. Within weeks they can mutate, altering their chemical makeup in order to prevent the absorption of the DNA-killing chemical.

In the same way, Satan manipulates minds and hearts to get teenagers to resist biblical counsel and sound judgment. Second Timothy 4:3–4 says, "For the time will come when they will not endure sound doctrine, but according to their own desires, because they have itching ears, they will heap up for themselves teachers; and they will turn their ears away from the truth, and be turned aside to fables." Even though you are giving your child sound counsel—"treating" the problem correctly—and even though she is experiencing pain, she will continue to resist. The spiritual onslaught has made it difficult for her to receive the things of God. Satan will anesthetize a child's heart against all good counsel, and if you don't see this happening, you will be in the dark as to how to help your child.

LIE #5: The wild child truly understands and fears the consequences of his or her actions.

Satan is a master at getting people to think there will be no consequences for their actions. He convinced Adam and Eve to disobey God by telling them that they would suffer no consequences. Not only would they not be punished for eating from the fruit tree, but they would be like God and control their own destiny. He uses the same lie on the wild child, telling her that she is in control with little or no consequences to worry about. Pray that your child would come to realize the consequences of her actions, not only on herself but also on those who are closest to her.

If the doctor does not know how cancer responds in certain situations, he will not be able to stay one step ahead of it in the treatment process. The doctor will try to anticipate what the cancer might do while he attempts to destroy it before it destroys the patient.

As you know by now, there is an architect behind the wild child's cancer: it is Satan. When he attacks your wild child, he is using a well-thought-out plan. The more you know about Satan's strategies, the better able you will be to devise a counterattack. Keep in mind, however, that Satan has his sights on you, too. He wants nothing less than to disrupt and destroy your family and your parenting ability.

You must believe that Satan is scheming and making evil plans specifically for your child. I want to use this chapter to give you more insights into how Satan thinks and operates. There is a method to his madness, and I hope that you will better understand what's happening with your child and what may lie ahead.

LIE #6: Satan is not involved in the details of your life.

It's a mistake to think that Satan isn't interested in destroying you or your family. He'll try to take advantage of seemingly small incidents or insecurities. He'll even attack strongholds, like he did with Job thousands of years ago.

Job was considered a great man with godly character. Yet Satan tried to destroy Job's relationship with God by accusing Job of serving God for selfish purposes. Satan was going to accuse Job of being a hypocrite, someone who would curse God if things didn't go his way. But God defended Job's integrity, saying that nothing could shake Job's faith.

Satan's strategy has several components, which we will examine in the next few pages in order to gain valuable insight about his access in and knowledge of our lives today.

It was just over fifteen years ago that Satan began his attack on the Olson family. It didn't matter that Tom and Cynthia loved the Lord and were serving Him as missionaries in Spain. Satan was out to ruin their faith. Unbeknownst to Tom and Cynthia, a boy from the church in Spain had begun sexually molesting their six-year-old daughter, Sarah (the family's names have been changed). Because Sarah was so young and scared, she never reported it. She'd cry for hours each day, but still kept the abuse a secret. Her parents didn't know what was wrong; they thought she was upset about being in a foreign land, away from her friends. But no matter how much they questioned Sarah, they never got an answer. In fact, it wasn't until ten years later, when other problems surfaced, that they learned how Satan was attacking their family.

Children are one of Satan's favorite targets, because he knows how much they mean to us. Even when they are safe, he will cloud our vision of reality and place thoughts of fear or discouragement in our minds. He will make us worry excessively about our children. Consequently, it's easy to begin placing unfair restrictions on their lives. He will trick you into accusing your child of doing things that she would never dream of doing. That doesn't mean every concern you have about your child is the result of Satan's lies. I don't want to cause you to second-guess yourself or God's leading. A parent's concerns are often justified. In addition, we have the right and responsibility to follow every lead or hunch we have.

Still, we must always keep in mind that the Evil One is at work, constantly trying to make a level-one problem into a level-two, -three, or -four crisis. This is his responsibility, and he is good at it. He is so good that it can be difficult to tell the difference between his lies and reality. This is why prayer is so important.

John 8:32 says, "And you shall know the truth, and the

truth shall make you free." Through prayer you can know the truth of God as it pertains to each and every situation concerning your child. Knowing the truth about what is going on will set you free from unnecessary worry and stress. It will set you free from falsely judging your child. It will set you free to experience the peace of God. Let's face it, when you have lie-based thoughts and assumptions floating around in your head, it is hard not to allow them to affect your feelings and how you treat your family or others.

If you fail to acknowledge Satan's role in your stress and worry, it's easy to blame all of it on your wild child. In addition to magnifying her problems, this will cause you even greater resentment for the pain she's brought to the family.

Not only can Satan infiltrate your life, he has a strong desire to do it. If you think he has no interest in you and your family, you are wrong. Any time Satan can get someone to turn his or her back on God, it is a victory for him, especially when it involves someone who claims to already belong to God. As we learn in 1 Peter 5:8: "Be sober, be vigilant; because your adversary the devil walks about like a roaring lion, seeking whom he may devour."

Satan hates you and your family, and he has plenty of demons working for him in a very organized manner that will do anything for him. You might have thought Satan's sole intent was to ruin the life of your child. Or to ruin your relationship with your child and the unity of your family. Well, his aim is bigger. Allow me to explain it this way.

Satan speaks three times in the Bible. The first time is when he challenged Adam and Eve on what God actually said concerning the Tree of Knowledge of Good and Evil. " 'Has God indeed said, "You shall not eat of every tree of the garden"?' " (Genesis 3:1). Eve explained that they could eat from all the trees except one. But Satan, as usual, had a well-prepared answer. " 'You will not surely die. For God knows that in the day you eat of it your eyes will be opened, and you will be like God, knowing good and evil' " (vv. 4–5). Basically, Satan was accusing God of holding out on them. His motive was not only to get them to eat the fruit but also to turn them against God, and it worked. Adam and Eve ate the forbidden fruit and found themselves kicked out of the garden. The intimate fellowship they had with God was broken.

In the book of Matthew, Satan speaks again, this time trying to get Jesus to worship him. "Again, the devil took Him up on an exceedingly high mountain, and showed Him all the kingdoms of the world and their glory. And he said to Him, 'All these things I will give You if You will fall down and worship me' " (Matthew 4:8–9). But in verse 10, Jesus shows us the correct response. "Then Jesus said to him, 'Away with you, Satan! For it is written, "You shall worship the Lord your God, and Him only you shall serve." ' " Satan's motive was to destroy the relationship between Jesus and His father by securing Jesus' worship.

In the book of Job, we read how Satan challenged God to believe that Job was only honoring God because God had blessed him. Satan asks, " 'Does Job fear God for nothing? Have You not made a hedge around him, around his household, and around all that he has on every side? You have blessed the work of his hands, and his possessions have increased in the land. But now, stretch out Your hand and touch all that he has, and he will surely curse You to Your face!' " (Job 1:9–11).

In this instance, Satan's motive was to get God to turn against humankind. But in each of the stories Satan's desired result was and remains the same. He wants to secure the worship of humankind for himself by destroying the relationship between God and people. Read Satan's words in Job 1:11 again: " 'But now, stretch out Your hand and touch all that he has, and he will surely curse You to Your face!' " This is how Satan wants to you to react to the pain and troubles caused by your child; he wants you to curse God. He wants you to blame God, to hold Him accountable for unanswered prayers concerning the healing of your wild child.

You might ask yourself, *What leverage does Satan have?* I will tell you. Your child's well-being is likely more dear to your heart than your trust in God. Satan wants you to curse God to His face. This was his plan with Job. Satan was banking on the idea that Job's wealth was more important to him than his relationship with God. He was hoping Job would begin blaming God for his troubles, accusing God of not answering his prayers.

So how do we resist Satan's schemes? How does the wild child win her spiritual battle? It is only possible with God's help. And it takes more than mere knowledge of Him. It is within the context of a relationship with God that we are transformed and empowered to live a life pleasing to God, a life victorious against the devil.

In Luke 19, we read about the life-changing power of a relationship with God. Zacchaeus, a hated tax collector, climbs into a tree to see Jesus, but is called down by the Lord. Jesus wants to go to Zacchaeus' house. Zacchaeus welcomes Him in, and what happens next is the result of nothing but the establishment of a relationship. "Then Zacchaeus stood and said to the Lord, 'Look, Lord, I give half of my goods to the poor; and if I have taken anything from anyone by false accusation, I restore fourfold' " (verse 8). This is true repentance and only comes when someone has a personal encounter with the King of Kings.

LIE #7: The bad timing of the wild child's troubles is only a coincidence.

Satan's two-part strategy to destroy Job's relationship with God was to get him to curse God and blame Him for all of his problems. But how would Satan accomplish this? By raining down unimaginable pain on Job. One tragedy after another would strike Job. And Satan thought that sooner or later Job would yell "uncle," curse God, and worship the Evil One.

> Now there was a day when his sons and daughters were eating and drinking wine in their oldest brother's house; and a messenger came to Job and said, "The oxen were plowing and the donkeys feeding beside them, when the Sabeans raided them and took them away—indeed they have killed the servants with the edge of the sword; and I alone have escaped to tell you!"
>
> While he was still speaking, another also came and said, "The fire of God fell from heaven and burned up the sheep and the servants, and consumed them; and I alone have escaped to tell you!"
>
> While he was still speaking, another also came and said, "The Chaldeans formed three bands, raided the camels and took them away, yes, and killed the servants with the edge of the sword; and I alone have escaped to tell you!"
>
> While he was still speaking, another also came and said, "Your sons and daughters were eating and drinking wine in their oldest brother's house, and suddenly a great wind came from across the wilderness and struck the four corners of the house, and it fell on the young people, and they are dead; and I alone have escaped to tell you!" (Job 1:13–19).

If we review this sequence of events we will learn some

important insights about Satan's strategy, which will help you to learn more about what is happening to your family. First, when you read about someone running to tell Job about a tragedy, the Bible says that while the person was still speaking, another servant ran in to tell Job about another tragedy. This happened four times in the course of two minutes! In that brief time, Job learned that he had lost everything—his livelihood, his wealth, and all of his children.

When I study this passage, I read it this way: instead of saying, "While he was still speaking," it could read, "While Job was beginning to hurt." While his pain was still increasing, while his shock was settling in, another tragedy struck. This is what the Master of Disaster, the devil, was banking on. How could he maximize Job's pain and discouragement? How could he ensure that when the bad news was over, Job would curse God? By heaping it on.

This is one of Satan's favorite strategies; creating one problem after another. Has he done it to your family? How many times have things happened in such a crazy sequence that you have wondered if someone was out to get you? Times are already troublesome when . . . Bam! Your son gets in trouble in school . . . Boom! Your daughter gets pregnant . . . Zap! The police bring your son home. How many times have you thought to yourself, *Why now? When will it end?*

Let me tell you, your child is not planning it out. Most kids aren't that smart, that calculating. Only Satan is that evil.

Earlier in this chapter I told you about the Olson family and the abuse Sarah suffered as a young girl. True to form, that was only the beginning of Satan's attack. More problems emerged in her teenage years—all in the devil's perfect timing, so as to amplify their impact.

The Olsons had moved back to the States when Tom and

Cynthia received a distressing phone call from the Christian school that Sarah was attending. She was sixteen now, and still hadn't revealed anything about the abuse in Spain. Her friends had noticed that Sarah would force herself to throw up after eating. They realized that she was suffering from bulimia. Needless to say, her parents were overwhelmed with the news, but they immediately sought counseling for Sarah.

It was a painful time for the entire family, and Cynthia realized what could bring about relief: prayer. She began a forty-day fast, but as it progressed, she became very discouraged and considered ending the fast. Sarah was still going through hell, and the family was going down with her. Cynthia cried out to God, *What else do I need to do?* It was at this same time that . . . Bam! The Olsons found out that Cynthia's mother, who was living with them, had bone cancer. They nursed her for more than nine months, until she passed away.

Looking back on the experience, Cynthia realizes that through her fast, God was preparing her for the pain that was to come. Because rather than getting better, life for her daughter got worse.

As Sarah's counseling progressed, she began to comprehend all of the junk she had been holding inside. Four months after her grandmother's death, Sarah tried killing herself. In a misguided attempt to end her pain, she swallowed an entire bottle of Tylenol and passed out. In that same year, Cynthia had her gall bladder removed, and her son totaled his car in an accident. As I said, if it seems like troubles come in bunches by coincidence, you are mistaken. Satan has a very systematic plan to destroy your relationship with God.

LIE #8: All of your troubles are God's fault.

One of Satan's purposes for creating trials and tribulations is to get you to begin blaming God for those troubles, and this will certainly come into play in a family that has a wild child.

In Job's case, Satan predicted Job would curse God if his riches were taken away. Have you cursed God yet for your wild child's troubles? Have you blamed God? Have you asked why He is not answering your prayers? If your answer is yes, you are on your way to cursing God and worshiping Satan, giving the devil just what he wants—your allegiance. You might think the idea of your worshiping Satan is farfetched, but allow me to explain. Worship is a response of respect to someone. Whenever you give the devil's opinions and views credibility or consideration, it can be called worship, a response of respect. In his eyes, you are one step closer to becoming one of his faithful followers. So even though God has given our kids to us, we must not allow our love for our kids to interfere with our love for and trust in God. It is Satan's mission to get as many as he can to go to hell with him.

At times Tom and Cynthia fell prey to blaming God for their family's troubles. They thought they had raised their children right. They had spent lots of time with the kids, especially when they were younger. They had served God on the mission field. But none of this mattered to Satan.

As the Father of Lies, Satan has a lie for every situation. He'll feed your mind with questions designed to blame God. *Why, God? Why me? Why my child? I have done everything right; I am serving you.* Satan will show you other parents who are not doing the things you think make a good parent, yet they are not having the problems your family is facing.

It's going to be difficult, but remember that for every one of Satan's lies, God provides the truth through His Word, the Bible. You must, through prayer, fight Satan's lies with God's truth: "For the weapons of our warfare are not carnal but mighty in God for pulling down strongholds, casting down arguments and every high thing that exalts itself against the knowledge of God, bringing every thought into captivity to the obedience of Christ" (2 Corinthians 10:4–5).

LIE #9: Your child will never change.

Satan will tell you that no matter what you do, no matter how much you pray or go to church, your wild child will never change. He'll tempt you to examine everything you have done and declare, *If she were going to change, it would have happened by now.*

Hopelessness is one of the devil's specialties. In the book of Mark, we read that he tried using it against Jairus, who had come to Jesus to heal his sick daughter. "While [Jesus] was still speaking, some came from the ruler of the synagogue's house, who said, 'Your daughter is dead. Why trouble the Teacher any further?' As soon as Jesus heard the word that was spoken, He said to the ruler of the synagogue, 'Do not be afraid; only believe' " (Mark 5:35–36).

When everything looks hopeless, remember Luke 18:27: "The things which are impossible with men are possible with God." As soon as you are ready to give up, look up and ask God for help and direction. Don't make a move until then.

LIE #10: The situation surrounding the wild child will never change.

Not only will Satan try to convince you that your wild child's life is hopeless, he will tell you that your family life will never improve or be normal. Your child's friends will continue to cause problems. You will never get over the pain. Sleepless nights and worry-filled days won't end. You will always be in a crisis-management mode.

As I said earlier, Satan is a master at turning level-one problems into level-four crises. With more than six billion people in this world, he wants you to think that your family is stuck with the same two, five, or ten people who are ruining the life of your wild child. He does not want you to think outside the lonely, fear-filled box that he intends for your mind and heart.

When you're attacked by Satan's lies, stand on God's promise: "Heaven and earth will pass away, but My words will by no means pass away" (Mark 13:31). Yes, even hard times will eventually end, but God's promises and faithfulness will never pass away. God can do anything He wants to do, whenever He wants to do it.

LIE #11: You are a failure as a parent.

Satan will challenge you with questions about your parenting. *What did I do to make my child turn out this way? Did I spend too little time with her? Too much time? Did I love her too little? Was I too harsh in my discipline?*

My friends, no matter how well we have done as parents, there is always something that could have been handled better. If we dwell too much on the past, it will drive us crazy. It is good to reevaluate situations and figure out how to do things better, but that is not the devil's intent. He wants you to beat yourself up and condemn yourself into depression and guilt. If that happens, trust me, it is from Satan and should be rebuked in prayer. In addition, no good thing is going to come from worrying and crying over what could have happened yesterday.

Matthew 6:34 says, "Therefore do not worry about tomorrow, for tomorrow will worry about its own things. Sufficient for the day is its own trouble." This verse also applies to our past. If God tells us not to worry about tomorrow, which, God willing, is something we are going to face and live through, how much more should we not worry about yesterday, which is already gone, never to return.

Takes notes on past situations, and if you have fallen short in how you handled things, commit to doing a better job tomorrow. This is what confession and repentance is all about. God is not in the business of punishing people who repent. He is into restoration.

What lies has Satan told you? Write them down and begin comparing those lies to the truth of God's Word. Search the Scriptures for verses that give you hope against those lies. For Cynthia, peace came to her as she faithfully prayed for Sarah and the rest of the family. In the midst of so many challenges, you might think peace would be nowhere to be found. But the Bible says that God provides love that surpasses all understanding, a peace the world cannot provide (Ephesians 3:19).

Job had this peace. He continued to trust and worship God when every earthly thing he knew was taken away. He honored God in good and bad times: "Then Job arose and tore his robe and shaved his head, and he fell to the ground and worshiped. And he said: 'Naked I came from my mother's womb, and naked shall I return there. The Lord gave, and the Lord has taken away; blessed be the name of the Lord' " (Job 1:20–21).

In all of this, Job did not sin or charge God with wrong. What was his secret? How could a man who had lost everything, only moments later respond in this way? It was not because of his wealth. His strength did not come from his large family. The answer is revealed in two earlier verses: "There was a man in the land of Uz, whose name was Job; and that man was blameless and upright, and one who feared God and shunned evil. . . . Then the Lord said to Satan, 'Have you considered My servant Job, that there is none like him on the earth, a blameless and upright man, one who fears God and shuns evil?' " (1:1, 8).

Job was a man who feared God with all his heart. He had a powerful relationship with God. This is going to be your most powerful weapon in dealing with your wild child and the wild force behind her. Only then will you be able to discern the nature of the spiritual battle going on in your family. Only then will you be able secure the peace that passes all understanding. Only then will you be able to run quickly to the strong tower for refuge amid the onslaughts of discouragement that Satan is sure to send your way.

Review Questions

1. In what areas of your life has Satan's access caused the most pain?
2. What lies has the devil been telling you about your situation?
3. What biblical truths refute those lies?
4. Have you cursed or blamed God yet? If so, what are you blaming Him for?
5. What verses counteract your accusations?

Chemo-Prayers Time

Lie #5: The wild child truly understands and fears the consequences of his or her actions.

Dear Lord, thank you for your Word. I pray that I would realize that Satan has lied to my wild child just like when he told Adam and Eve they would not die if they disobeyed God.

Lie #6: Satan is not involved in the details of your life.

Dear Lord, thank you for your Word. I pray that I will be given the discernment to be aware of Satan's influence in my life and my family's. More importantly, please give me the confidence to trust that you will defeat and frustrate the plans of the devil. I know, God, that you have more power than Satan to influence my life and my child's. I understand that it is my responsibility to surrender all of my fears and concerns to you. I know that I must obey James 4:7–8, which says, "Therefore submit to God. Resist the devil and he will flee from you. Draw near to God and He will draw near to you."

Lie #7: The bad timing of the wild child's troubles is only a coincidence.

Dear Lord, thank you for your faithfulness in my life. I know that Satan is very smart and deceptive. I know that Satan's plan is to maximize the pain and frustration I feel about my child. But I also believe that you are smarter than the devil and that you can provide the wisdom I need to spiritually prepare for his wiles. Please give me the wisdom and discipline to be faithful to what is commanded in Ephesians 6:10–11, which says, "Finally, my brethren, be strong in the Lord and in the power of His might. Put on the whole armor of God, that you may be able to stand against the wiles of the devil."

Lie #8: All of your troubles are God's fault.

Dear Lord, thank you for your Word. Please forgive me for blaming you for my family's troubles. I know that Satan wants me to turn away from you and to worship him instead. Protect my mind and heart from losing trust in your faithfulness and show me how to use your truth to fight Satan's lies. Help me to remember to live like Job, who continued to worship you even when times were terrible.

Lie #9: Your child will never change.

Dear Lord, thank you for your Word. Thank you for showing from your Word that Satan has incredible access into my life.

Now I am aware that I need to pray over every aspect of my life and that of my child's. I know that 2 Corinthians 5:17 says that if anyone is in Christ, he is a new creature, the old is gone and the new has come. Please bring the new into the life of my child.

Lie #10: The situation surrounding the wild child will never change.

Dear Lord, I realize that when you say the "old is gone and the new has come," this not only applies to the spiritual condition of someone's life but also to the circumstances in that life. I believe that you have the desire and power to change the circumstances surrounding the life of my child. I know that you have power over all things, including the friends and other negative influences in my child's life. Thank you for faithfully being involved in all areas of our family's life.

Lie #11: You are a failure as a parent.

Dear Lord, thank you for your Word. Thank you for showing me that there is always hope for a better tomorrow. Your Word says in Romans 8:31 that if you are for me, no one can be against me. I will hold on to that promise and believe that you will change the circumstances concerning my child. The Bible also says that nothing is impossible with God. I know that you can change the life of my child, so I will never give up hope. Help me to also hold on to that hope when I start to think I am a failure. I believe that you will forgive my wrongs and bring about the necessary changes in me.

Chapter Three

ONE WILD WEAPON: PRAYER

WHEN SOMEONE IS diagnosed with cancer, countless things race through that person's mind. Some people go into a stage of denial, thinking it's not very serious and that they will beat it. Others immediately panic, fearing the worst.

When Caroline discovered she had cancer, her first response was, *This is not going to be that bad. God can handle it.* But when she learned the cancer had entered her lymph system, her sense of urgency was heightened. It had truly become a life-and-death issue, especially after it progressed to her spinal cord. At that point, Caroline was told she had only six months to live. No human could heal her. No one had ever survived her particular type of cancer.

Caroline decided not to become a cancer expert but a God expert. She would never find a cure herself, but she would seek the One who could heal her, the Great Physician. The cancer was trying to kill her, and chemotherapy was her doctor's weapon of choice, but Caroline's number one weapon was prayer.

As I have emphasized throughout this book, Satan is your enemy and prayer is your weapon. Second Corinthians 10:4 says, "For the weapons of our warfare are not carnal but mighty in God for pulling down strongholds." Nothing is going to change your child's heart like fervent prayer. But what exactly is prayer, and how can you use it to your fullest advantage?

One day a little boy was walking through a park, blowing soapy bubbles through one of those rings on a stick. After five minutes of sending hundreds of bubbles into the air, he sat down with his mother. Just before getting up to play with some friends, he looked up to find bubbles floating from the sky. Several bubbles landed on him with a pop. To his delight, they were more than fun. They filled him with a kind of peace. He decided to blow more bubbles. And sure enough, they came back down to thrill him again. Then he ran to get one of those giant bubble blowers. Before long, huge bubbles were raining down, overwhelming him with more happiness than he could handle.

I tell this little story to illustrate that when you pray, you are sending God bubbles of requests, problems, and concerns as well as praise, thanks, and love. In return, He sends back not only information but also power, joy, patience, and love. God communicates according to His good pleasure and eternal will as it pertains to our lives. Many people think prayer is simply asking God for things they want. Other people only go to God in times of crisis. God always listens, but prayer should and needs to be so much more than this. Prayer is communication with God. It is communicating your requests, needs, and struggles with God, and then letting Him communicate His messages and blessings to you.

God created prayer as the only way we can communicate with Him. Yes, our lives and our actions reflect our trust and commitment to Him, but when it comes to communicating directly with God, prayer is the tool. Through prayer we can summon His assistance and action on our behalf. For Jesus said in John 14:13, "And whatever you ask in My name, that I will do, that the Father may be glorified in the Son." Moses prayed for God to part the Red Sea, and He did it. Prayer is what Elijah used to stop the rain for three and a half years. Prayer is how Jesus raised the twelve-year-old girl from the dead and how He healed the blind man.

When you get on your knees to pray for your wild child, you need to believe that miracles are possible for his life. Hebrews 11:1 says, "Now faith is the substance of things hoped for, the evidence of things not seen." If you do not have faith, you should not even pray. You must expect your prayers to be answered. You must expect the unexpected, because God is a miracle worker. You might be praying for something that is impossible with man, but God is willing to do the *Himpossible* for you and your family. God wants to amaze us. He wants to teach us many things about our lives and our children. In Jeremiah 33:3, He says, "Call to Me, and I will answer you, and show you great and mighty things, which you do not know."

The Bible tells us that people were amazed by the miracles Jesus performed while on earth. Some, however, did not believe His miracles were of God. In the third chapter of Mark, Jesus was accused of casting out devils by the power of Satan. But Jesus clearly says that His healing works actually undo the works of the devil. "No one can enter a strong man's house and plunder his goods, unless he first binds the strong man, and then he will plunder his house" (v. 27).

No one can undo the devil's work or overcome his influence unless they first bind the devil. This does not mean that if you are sick, Satan is tormenting you. But it does mean that the Holy Spirit has power over everything pertaining to our lives, and that through the Holy Spirit, God can bring about any change He desires. So when you pray, you must understand that you are binding the Strong Man, the one whose spiritual influence is nothing but evil. He is behind your child's rebelliousness. Satan is keeping your child in bondage, away from the freedom he so desperately needs.

LIE #12: Prayers are just as effective whether they are organized or not.

Have you ever had a conversation with someone who talked in circles? Or someone who couldn't stick to one subject for more than two sentences? Wasn't it irritating?

It is true that God will hear, respect, and respond to your prayers no matter what order they are in. However, the more organized and focused you are when you talk with God, the more effective your prayers will be.

Before I present specific prayer strategies for parenting a wild child, I want to give you a brief overview on how to pray. When you pray, it is important to be focused. I find it helps to use the acrostic AWCIPA. Each letter represents a topic of prayer.

A — Admire God, give thanks
W — Wait on the Lord in silence
C — Confess your sins to the Lord
I — Intercede for others

P — Petition, pray for yourself

A — Admire, thank God again

It is very important to pray with focus, one letter or topic at a time. Spending five to ten minutes on each topic will result in thirty to sixty minutes of focused prayer. Set aside a specific time to communicate with the Father on a regular basis. To me, morning is as good as any other time.

A is for admiring and thanking God. Praising Him is an excellent way to begin your prayers, because no matter what your crisis is, it could be worse. In addition, there are always many things to be thankful for.

W is waiting before the Lord in silence. Psalm 46:10 tells us to be still and know that He is God. Time spent sitting quietly before the Lord will help you place Him back on the throne of your heart. Many times the whirlwind of crisis after crisis can cause us to lose focus on who is really in charge. Satan would love for you to begin to think that Mr. Crisis is in charge. Sit quietly before God and allow Him to speak to you.

C is for confessing your sins before the Lord. Pour out your heart to Him. *Search me, O God. . . .*

I stands for intercession, the next step in a focused prayer. Since intercessory prayer is the focus of this chapter, I will introduce this vital topic in the next section.

P is for petition, praying for our own personal needs. Unfortunately, this is usually the first and main thing we do when we pray. *Dear God, give me this and give me that.* By following the AWCIPA prayer format, you save your own personal needs until the end. By putting God and the needs of others first, you will find that your petitions will be much more humble in nature.

A stands for admire God—to close your prayer with more thanksgiving and praise. Philippians 4:6 says, "Be anxious for nothing, but in everything by prayer and supplication, with thanksgiving, let your requests be made known to God." In all things, remember to thank God.

The key to all of this is to pray in one category at a time. Try not to ramble through all of your requests, complaints, and thanks at the same time. This is not so much for God's sake, but yours. Keeping a journal is also a tremendous help when trying to stay focused. Writing down what God is telling you, in addition to recording your prayer requests and answers, is a powerful way to appreciate what God is doing in your life.

Another way of keeping your prayers focused is by inserting your child's name in Scripture. Since one of the key components to prayers being answered is their biblical accuracy, nothing could be more powerful. Look up verses that apply to your child's needs, or even your own needs. Then write the verse out and personalize it with your child's name. For example, in John 17:15, Jesus says, "I do not pray that You should take them out of the world, but that You should keep them from the evil one." To focus this verse on your child, replace the word "them" with your child's name. "I do not pray that You should take [child's name] out of the world, but that You should keep [him/her] from the evil one."

Even if there is no natural place for a name, be creative. For example, 1 Corinthians 6:18 is perfect for someone struggling with sexual impurity: "Flee sexual immorality. Every sin that a man does is outside the body, but he who commits sexual immorality sins against his own body." Insert your child's name, and it reads something like this: "Lord, I pray that [child's name] would flee sexual immorality. Every sin that a man does is outside the body, but he who commits sexual immorality sins against his own body."

This practice is also a great way to memorize Scripture while at the same time lifting your child up in prayer.

LIE #13: Praying for others won't work unless they have a desire to change.

It has been interesting to watch the many court cases on television in recent years. The most famous, of course, was the O. J. Simpson trial. Even though it happened many years ago, the courtroom battles are still fresh in our minds. With the advent of Court TV, many of us have become armchair lawyers, casting our own judgments in televised cases.

These cases probably wouldn't be broadcast if there weren't money to be made, but they do help educate viewers about the legal system. Many legal terms and procedures have been brought to light. We've also learned more about the role of the judge, the jury, and the lawyers. Defense lawyers fascinate me the most. They defend their clients before a judge and, more importantly, a jury, the people who actually decide whether the defendant is innocent or guilty. The jury also decides in large part the degree of punishment for this person. Defense attorneys, using relevant facts, try to convince a jury that their client is innocent. Sometimes they ask for mercy in the sentencing.

When it comes to the wild child and prayer, you are the defense attorney. You are the child's advocate, his trial lawyer, pleading his case before the Judge.

The Bible calls this intercession; the act of petitioning God, through prayer, on behalf of another person or group. When you intercede, you are pleading with God on behalf of your child. It is during this time that you will charge against the spiritual forces of darkness in his life with the most powerful weapon known to humankind: prayer. Satan will try to get you to believe that intercessory prayer doesn't work—especially in the case of a wild child who isn't willing to change—but believe this: Powerful intercession can turn a heart. Proverbs 21:1 says, "The king's heart is in the hand of the Lord, like the rivers of water; He turns it wherever He wishes." God can change a heart, but someone must ask and plead for that heart.

Our sinful nature, often displayed by rebellious behavior, separates us from God. It has always been necessary, therefore, for righteous individuals to go before God to seek reconciliation between Him and His fallen creation. On behalf of your child, you are to argue his case in heaven's court. You must be the one who brings his case to court to ask for mercy and grace.

Interceding for someone is an awesome gift, but it can also be intimidating. Thankfully, we have a righteous advocate in heaven: Jesus. And He is arguing our case before the Father. First John 2:1 says, "My little children, these things I write to you, that you may not sin. And if anyone sins, we have an Advocate with the Father, Jesus Christ the righteous." There are also several instances in the Bible when Jesus prayed for people. In John 17, He prayed for His disciples and the world, and in Luke 22, He prayed for Peter.

This passage in Luke contains key insights on intercession. Jesus is speaking to Peter about how Peter will soon disown Him.

> "Simon, Simon! Indeed, Satan has asked for you, that he may sift you as wheat. But I have prayed for you, that your faith should not fail; and when you have returned to Me, strengthen your brethren."
>
> But he said to Him, "Lord, I am ready to go with You, both to prison and to death."
>
> Then He said, "I tell you, Peter, the rooster shall not

crow this day before you will deny three times that you know Me." (Luke 22:31–34)

Jesus was aware of Satan's desire to destroy Peter. And He also knew Peter would be unable to resist the devil. Read again what Jesus said: "Peter, the rooster shall not crow this day before you will deny . . . Me." We all know the story. Peter denied and even cursed Jesus' name three times that very night.

Jesus understands the wiles of the devil. First Peter 5:8 says, "Your adversary the devil walks about like a roaring lion, seeking whom he may devour." Satan has weapons that your child cannot resist unless he is supernaturally undergirded by prayer. These weapons are designed to bring unbelievable temptation into his life. Nothing is beyond the scope of the Evil One's imagination.

Do you believe that Satan is trying to destroy your child? Rather than thinking that your child has problems that will destroy him, do you recognize that Satan is implementing a well-thought-out plan to destroy your child? As I've said before, Satan's influence does not excuse your child from being responsible for his actions, but it should affect the way you approach the problem.

In Mark 9, we read about a father who had no doubt that Satan was behind his son's troubles. When Jesus asked the man how long the boy had been tormented, he replied, "And often he has thrown him both into the fire and into the water to destroy him. But if You can do anything, have compassion on us and help us" (v. 22). This father also knew that Jesus was his son's only hope.

LIE #14: If my wild child's behavior is not improving, my prayers must not be working.

Satan wants you to be discouraged, to stop praying if you're not seeing better results. It's easy to get caught up with outside appearances. But the focus of your prayers should not be that your child improves his behavior. Rather, you need to pray that your child becomes one with God.

The wild child will always say one thing but do another. He will promise not to lie, cheat, and steal. And you will sit back and watch your child do exactly what he promised not to do—sometimes that very night—just like Jesus did when Peter vowed never to deny Him.

Brent has been disappointing his parents for quite some time. It started when they caught him smoking pot on several occasions. Back then, he had little interest in going to church, and he was generally the center of family disruptions. Eventually, he was imprisoned for possessing stolen property and breaking probation.

Brent has broken countless promises to change and avoid trouble, and he continues to fall further and further from the Lord. His parents, though, have a very spiritual and biblically based viewpoint. They know that God's plan takes time. And they are confident that one day their son will know Christ and straighten his life out.

When you experience broken promises in your family, keep your eyes on the big picture. Try to have the mind of Christ. He wasn't discouraged or misled by Peter's promise not to deny Him. Instead, Christ prayed that Peter would maintain a steadfast faith. This is an important point. Jesus did not ask Peter to resist denying Him that night. Rather, He prayed that Peter's faith would not fail. Of course, Jesus would have been pleased if Peter had stood strong and proclaimed Him. But long-term, Peter's experience was valuable in his life.

Again, Jesus did not focus on Peter's behavior that very night, but on his long-term relationship with God. This heavenly desire is also evident when Jesus meets with His disciples for the last time and prays for them and for the world. His over-riding concern was for unity with Him and with the Father:

> "I pray for them. I do not pray for the world but for those whom You have given Me, for they are Yours. And all Mine are Yours, and Yours are Mine, and I am glorified in them. Now I am no longer in the world, but these are in the world, and I come to You. Holy Father, keep through Your name those whom You have given Me, that they may be one as We are." (John 17:9–11)

In verses 20–21, Jesus aims His prayer at nonbelievers: "I do not pray for these alone, but also for those who will believe in Me through their word; that they all may be one, as You, Father, are in Me, and I in You; that they also may be one in Us, that the world may believe that You sent Me."

The foundation of your prayers should be focused not on changing your child's actions, but in securing his position in heaven. Not on outward behavior, but on inward hope. Don't get me wrong; it is very important to pray for a change in be-havior. But it is more important and life-changing for the wild child to have a faith and trust in God. Keep in mind that a child's behavior, as bad as it can be, may indicate his lack of love for God, but it does not indicate God's lack of love for the child. God is anxiously waiting for your child to turn back to Him, just as you are.

It's all the more important to focus your prayers on inward hope, because teenagers are masters of disguise and deception. They can hide their pain with a smile.

Brian found this out the hard way. He thought his fifteen-year-old daughter was a happy child. She was pleasant to be around, always smiling and laughing. But he learned this was a cover-up the day he walked into her bedroom and found her burning her hand over a candle. Once he composed himself, he asked her what was going on. "Dad, there are lots of dark things in my life you don't know about, and you don't want to know." It took a while, but Brian learned that his daughter was suffering from bulimia. Months of counseling followed, which uncovered many other related issues.

Kids can fake anything they want to fake. When they go to school, they can become who they want to be to fit the circumstances. As teenagers, they are still trying to figure out who they are and will try different versions of themselves in their attempt to fit in.

Instead of praying that your child will stop drinking, pray that he will begin reading the Bible. Instead of focusing your prayers on your child's ceasing to look for love through sex, pray that he would look for love in a relationship with Jesus. Instead of focusing on a child's need to stop hungering for the praise of his friends, pray that he would hunger and thirst for righteousness. Pray that in the midst of all that your child is going through, the flicker of faith will not go out.

But what if there never was a flicker of faith? Even for that child, pray that one day he will be one with the Father as you are one with Him. This prayer will actually be the prayer for his salvation. And when he accepts and trusts Christ, your other prayer requests will be answered. That's because God promises to fulfill our needs when we seek to please Him and allow Him control of our lives: "But seek first the kingdom of God and His righteousness, and all these things shall be added to you" (Matthew 6:33).

If the wild child seeks, desires, and apprehends the kingdom of God in his life, God promises to give him and thus the child's family everything they will ever need. If his faith is intact and there is a flicker of belief in God, in time this will turn into a flame, a flame that will change his heart.

Sanya's parents had done their best to introduce Sanya and their other children to the Lord. And for the first part of Sanya's life, she was the typical sweet, happy kid. But then things changed—suddenly. Out of nowhere she acquired a quick temper toward her parents, and became uncharacteristically rude. She stopped saying good-bye when they dropped her off at school. They thought Sanya's rebellion was somehow related to going to a new school; and every once in a while she'd make a comment about not being able to be as godly as her sisters. But still the sudden change was puzzling. The whole family went to a counselor for months, but Sanya's heart was hard toward the process. They even sent her to a special program in Canada for eighteen months, but she came home unchanged.

Her parents' frustration grew. Things got to the point of becoming violent. One day Sanya's mom slapped her, and without hesitation Sanya slapped her back. In desperation, her parents decided to fast and pray for their kids. Oh, they had been praying for their kids like most of us do: *Dear God, please keep our kids pure; bless them . . . blah, blah, blah.* But now it was time for war. Sanya's parents realized that they needed to wage a serious, relentless battle in the heavenly places.

Matthew 21:22 says, "And whatever things you ask in prayer, believing, you will receive." This verse means exactly what it says. Whatever you ask for according to the will of God, in Jesus' name, you will receive if you believe. At the same time, Jesus has the freedom, whether we ask Him or not, to do whatever He wants to do, whenever He wants to do it, and in any way that He wants to do it. So if you are going to place your trust in God through prayer, which is my recommendation, you must be willing to accept His answers. This is exactly what Sanya's parents did. Nothing else had worked, so they surrendered their daughter to God and began to fast and pray for her.

Then the totally unexpected happened.

Sanya was diagnosed with leukemia. She was eighteen years old. But her parents accepted it, saying, "This is of the Lord." No parent wants his or her child to develop cancer. But Sanya's mom and dad were in tune with God's will and trusted His sovereignty. They believed that God can put you in a place spiritually and emotionally where you are ready to accept anything He gives you in order to fulfill His will and His plan in the life of your child.

After months of treatments, prayers, and love, Sanya's cancer was gone, and her faith and trust in God was renewed. She is now back to her old self, and she wants to work with kids who have cancer. Even so, her parents have not stopped praying for her, not only to prevent the cancer from returning but also that her heart would be turned on for the Lord. (During the peak of their family's problems, they realized that Sanya's distance from God had become the main issue.)

It is vitally important to *keep the main thing the main thing*. So when you pray, pray that your child will walk with God. How would you feel if he or she stopped getting high, stopped cursing, or stopped sleeping around—but went to hell?

LIE #15: All I need to do is pray, and everything will work out for good.

Many people think, *Since I am saved, and a relatively good person, everything will work out for good*. They point to the promise found in Romans 8:28, which says, "And we know that all things work together for good to those who love God, to those who are the called according to His purpose." But if you read this verse carefully, there is a condition to be met for things to work out for good: you must love God.

Satan wants you to simply trust the first part of the verse without feeling a responsibility to fulfill the second part. Do you love God? What does it mean to love God?

First John 5:3 tells us, "For this is the love of God, that we keep His commandments. And His commandments are not burdensome." In other words, as you pray for your wild child, God is going to give you direction, wisdom, and orders, but the key to things working out for good is that you obey God. You can pray all day, but if you do not obey what God says, your experience will be different from the person who does obey. It is not only important to commit yourself to being obedient but also to listen carefully in your prayer times for what God wants you to be obedient about.

Your willingness to deny yourself and to pick up your cross and follow Him is going to play the biggest role in your intercession process. The Bible teaches us that more than any prayer Jesus might have prayed, being crucified on the cross was his ultimate act of intercession. In the same way, your flesh must be crucified in order to be an effective intercessor. Your life must be sanctified, and His life, through yours, must be glorified in order for your prayers to be effective.

When you watch your son or your daughter deny Christ with their life, remember that Jesus is praying that they will be one with Him. He is praying that when your child returns to Him, he or she will be able to encourage others. Your child's experiences will be used for good in someone else's life. Until then, keep praying and keep obeying God. Don't forget the calling He has on your life. What Satan intends for evil, God will use for good.

LIE #16: God knows my needs; therefore, I don't need to pray about specific details.

After a chapel service with the NFL's Chicago Bears, a player asked me whether he had to ask God for exactly what he wanted, since God already knew the desires of his heart. He thought it would be selfish to list everything he wanted. I told him that God wants to hear our prayers and our desires, and it is important to be very specific with our requests. As Psalm 37: 4 says, "Delight yourself also in the Lord, and He shall give you the desires of your heart." This truth could not have been more evident than during a conference I spoke at for Moms In Touch International.

Moms In Touch is a ministry whose purpose is to mobilize moms to pray for kids in schools. Besides the fact that the group's founder and president, Fern Nichols, is a dear friend, I jumped at the opportunity to speak to thirteen hundred praying women. I could only imagine the power of those women and the spirit that would fill the auditorium. And just as I thought, it was powerful. Women from all over the world attended.

As the night progressed, and Fern gave her opening speech, the enthusiasm in the room was overwhelming. With every praise report of changed lives, cheers rang out. But the loudest cheer came when Fern began asking women about the answered prayers they had seen in their children's lives. With the enthusiasm of a football coach giving a half-time speech, Fern asked, "How many moms have had your prayers answered? Have seen that girlfriend or boyfriend taken out of your child's life?" Hundreds of women stood and cheered.

"How many have seen prodigals get off the streets, come home, and go back to church?" Hundreds more stood and cheered.

"How many moms have prayed and seen your children come to know Christ as their Savior?" Not only did these moms cheer but they also jumped to their feet, raised their arms, and screamed their praise.

These women knew what they had prayed for. They knew what results they were looking for. They knew and recorded in their hearts the answers that came. But most importantly, they believed that the changed lives of their children were the result of prayer.

You must know what you are praying for and be prepared to give the credit due His holy name. You must believe that prayer is your number one weapon against the spiritual cancer that is killing your child. If you are not keeping track of your requests, you will never know when God moves to answer those requests. You may ask God to give your child a desire to pray, but then forget your request. And when that day comes, and your child wants to pray, you will not be able to acknowledge the fact that God answered your prayers.

Review Questions

1. Have you been praying with focus, one topic at a time, or praying for everything under the sun?
2. Are you praying for a change in your child's behavior or for his or her faith in God?
3. Have your prayers brought about a change in *your* behavior?
4. Do you believe that prayer can change a heart?

Chemo-Prayers Time

Lie #12: Prayers are just as effective whether they are organized or not.

Dear Lord, thank you for your Word. Help me to pray in a way that helps me keep track of my requests. It is obvious that in the Lord's Prayer, you provide a model for prayer that has order and structure. Help my prayers to have both focus and power. I pray that I would learn to use your Word in my prayers, basing them on the truth of your promises.

Lie #13: Praying for others won't work unless they have a desire to change.

Dear Lord, thank you for your Word. I know Satan has the power to influence my child, but I know that your power to influence him/her is even greater. I pray for a changed heart in my child. Please give him/her a hunger and thirst for right-eousness. Today I would like to pray Psalm 51:10 over my child's life and attitude. "Create in [child's name] a clean heart, O God, and renew a steadfast spirit within him/her."

Lie #14: If my wild child's behavior is not improving, my prayers must not be working.

Dear Lord, thank you for your Word. I realize that your ways are not my ways. I realize that I don't see things as you do and that I should not try to judge the spiritual effectiveness of my prayers. I will continue to trust that in time you will answer my prayers.

Lie #15: All I need to do is pray, and everything will work out for good.

Dear Lord, thank your for your Word. I realize that I must be obedient in order for my prayers to be empowered. I know that all things work out for good for those who love you, and loving you is obeying you. James 5:16 says, "The effective, fervent prayer of a righteous man avails much." May I become a more obedient and righteous person.

Lie #16: God knows my needs; therefore, I don't need to pray about specific details.

Dear Lord, thank you for your Word. I realize that when I pray, I need to ask and be specific. I pray that I would be clearer about my requests. I know that this will require time and effort on my part to be more in tune with my desires, so I pray that you would guide me. Psalm 37:4 says that if I delight myself in you, you will give me the desires of my heart. Please grant me a yearning for you, so that I may receive those desires from your throne.

Chapter Four

WILD GUIDELINES: GET IN LINE

CAROLINE BECAME WEAKER and weaker as her cancer progressed. As the mother of four girls under the age of seven, her responsibilities were enormous, but she had less energy to do everyday things. She often felt nauseated and experienced times of vomiting. Her hair fell out, and parts of her body became very swollen. Sometimes Caroline felt like giving up, but with tears in her eyes she would vow, "My girls . . . I cannot leave my girls." She prayed for them daily, concerned about how they would get along without her. She prayed for the men that would come into their lives as they grew up, the friends they would meet, and their relationships with God.

As Caroline struggled with the side effects of her cancer treatment, her doctor considered two options. They could lower the level of chemotherapy, thus reducing its unwanted effects on the body. The problem is, chemotherapy works best when it is given in doses as high as the patient can endure. The lower the dose, the slower it kills the cancer. The other option was to begin immunotherapy, which is designed to strengthen the body's natural immune system and give it a fighting chance to kill the cancer on its own.

As we have said, each and every one of us is susceptible to cancer, because we all have the gene that can trigger the disease. And when proto-oncogenes are damaged, they can become cancerous. But since we don't all develop cancer, something else must be occurring in our body. That something else is the function of our immune system, which fights to shield our body from cancer. The white blood cells that make up our immune system are very familiar with the process of recognizing and defeating cancer. There are, of course, times when they cannot win the battle, but it is their job to protect us. In fact, the immune system is our first line of defense against all "enemies" of the body. Once our immune system encounters a disease or virus, it will read its DNA and form an antibody, or antidote, to defeat the virus the next time it sees it. This is the theory behind the use of vaccines for flu, measles, and chicken pox.

Obviously a strong immune system is important. The healthier we are—the better our diet, the more consistently we get enough rest, etc.—the stronger our immune system will be to prevent illness. And even if we do get sick, the immune system is still our best ally against disease.

When Caroline was diagnosed with cancer, her doctor prescribed several basic practices to help strengthen Caroline's immune system. He advised her to eat lots of fruits and vegetables, drink lots of water, and get plenty of rest. She was told to take the proper vitamins regularly and get a healthy amount of exercise and fresh air. And since Caroline's emotional and spiritual health would be just as important as her physical health, he encouraged things like lots of laughter.

When dealing with a wild child who is totally or partially out of control, it's important to get back to the basics and establish a strong first line of defense—a set of guidelines or rules for living in your home. These guidelines will be the basis for monitoring change and normalcy in the home. They will also help determine appropriate disciplinary actions. Having a clear set of guidelines for your child will also strengthen the overall health of the family, in part because it will reduce your stress by not having to try to figure out what to do in every situation. Preset rules and guidelines will help make those decisions for you.

LIE #17: Rules in the home will take the fun out of your relationship with your child.

Before a speaking appearance at a junior high school a while back, I decided to walk around the campus to get a feel for the place. My first impression was that the kids were out of control. I didn't know how I'd get them to settle down and listen to me. But when the principal walked through the schoolyard, she did something very simple yet profound. She grabbed about ten bright orange cones and set them across the ground. Once the cones were in place, she blew her whistle. The kids immediately knew what to do. They lined up inside the cones and waited for further direction. As long as the students remained within the boundaries, they were okay.

Regaining control of your home involves two phases: (1) setting boundaries for your wild child and the family, and (2) establishing proper discipline for wrong actions and rebellious behavior. I'll discuss discipline in the next chapter, but here I want to focus on family rules and guidelines.

One of Satan's favorite tricks is to get parents to think rules won't work. He might even tell you that rules would only add to the tension between you and your child. But appropriate, biblical rules are necessary for two reasons: (1) some will prevent children from behavior that will destroy their lives, and (2) others are designed to help children improve their lives.

I can't tell you what specific rules and guidelines your family needs, because every situation is different. However, the best way to start is to review the list you made in chapter 1 of behaviors you consider "wild" and then establish rules accordingly. As you do this, it's important to know that family rules should apply to everyone, not just the wild child. The rules must even apply to you as a parent. Also, you must be careful not to rob your children of all their freedoms. Remember, kids are kids—they need to live the life of a kid—so don't make rules that are simply impossible to keep.

Rules and guidelines should be balanced and drawn up with a positive attitude. As brothers and sisters in Christ, we are all under the authority of God and need to live in harmony with one another. And this can only happen if we all live under the grace and guidance of God.

Make sure your child understands that there are consequences for crossing the boundaries you have set. Often we parents can use our children's interests and desires as leverage. If your child really wants something—to participate in a sport, own a car, enjoy freedom to hang out with friends, go on a trip, etc.—let her know her special privilege can be taken away as a form of punishment. Although she'll probably claim it's unfair and try to manipulate you, stick to what you believe is the right decision.

Remember that you are in a spiritual battle with Satan—rules won't solve all of the problems. But by being strong, you will be well on the way to changing things around your house.

Our fourteen-year-old daughter has two loves: ballet and animals. There is also has one thing she hates: math. If she had her way, she would live, and take ballet lessons, at the zoo. And as far as I am concerned, ballet and animals are two noble interests.

One evening I overheard my daughter trying to get my wife to sign something from school. I stuck my nose into the conversation and asked to see the paper. She showed me a homework approval sheet, and I asked what it meant. (Don't ever sign anything without fully understanding what you are signing!) She said it was to show that we approved her homework that had been corrected. Well, I hadn't seen any homework, so guess what? I asked her to bring it to me. I soon found out why she hadn't shown us her work. Math worksheets showed grades of only 15 to 25 percent correct. Needless to say, the grades were unacceptable.

This happened to be the same day that we had given her a pet bird for a birthday present, something she had wanted for some time. "Do you understand that having a bird and taking ballet are privileges?" I asked. Then I got out her report card and we discussed her educational situation. I circled all of her grades and wrote next to them *my* expectations for each class. I told her the report card would serve as a contract between us. By the next term I expected *C*s to be turned into *B*s and *B*s into *A*s. If this didn't happen, she'd be pulled out of ballet. "What if I don't sign the contract?" she asked. "Then I will take you out of ballet *now*." I couldn't get out of the way fast enough as she grabbed for the pen. Still, as she began to sign the report card, she couldn't resist asking what would happen if she signed her sister's name. Can't blame a girl for trying.

The key to making rules work is that your child must know you are serious. She must know and believe that you will follow through with your promises and threats. However, establishing guidelines, or in this case, making a contract, isn't the end of your responsibilities. As parents, we want our children to win, to meet their goals and ours. Therefore, we need to help them succeed.

In my daughter's situation, I posted the report card where we could see it daily as a constant reminder of her agreement. I also made sure that she had the proper tutoring for classes in which she was struggling, such as math. We later researched colleges that offered ballet and found out their math requirements. All of this gave her more determination to work at improving her grades. In the end, the experience brought us closer together and forced me to be more involved in her education. The contract acted as an objective disciplinarian. There was an expectation, a timetable, and a consequence. It was very simple, but she knew her responsibilities. I didn't have to manage her every move. I just kept track of her progress as we had outlined it.

Nancy has also used parental leverage to enforce a rule in her family. Her sixteen-year-old son, Matthew, had started to argue with her and talk back. Since he had been saving his money to buy a car by Christmas, she let him know that for every time he talked back to her she would postpone the car purchase by one month. He hated the idea, but she has stuck to her decision. To make it work, however, Nancy has to follow through on the consequences. That is, if Matthew talks back, she has to actually postpone the purchase of the car. The rule seems to be working. Matthew thinks twice before opening his mouth. And once he gets the car, if the arguing starts up again, Nancy's leverage will be to take away his privilege of driving it.

LIE #18: Parents don't have a right to know and control everything that happens in the home.

God has given us our children and our homes and has commanded us to be the best stewards of them until He comes back. But as you know, Satan has many tricks up his sleeve to steal our children and our families. He will use even everyday things like cars, music, and friends to corrupt young people. For the rest of this chapter, I want to present nine areas of a teenager's life that are especially vulnerable to attack and ideas for how you can establish certain rules and guidelines to help protect your child. There are countless other danger areas, but paying attention to these will help you to start regaining control of your home and family life. And if your child breaks the rules, I've suggested some "wild" parent alternatives that are sure to make a statement!

1. Window Access

When we bought our house, I looked for certain features knowing that we would have children one day. For example, I checked out the yard and imagined them running around in it, wondering if a pool or swing set would fit. But when my wife delivered our first child, the home's windows suddenly became one of my biggest worries. I feared that someone would break in and take our daughter. Even though she was on the second floor, a patio cover outside her window would have provided enough access to someone who really wanted to get in and take her. In fact, not long after I considered this, I heard news that a little girl had been snatched this way and later murdered.

As children grow up, the question is not so much whether someone will come into their window to hurt them as who they will invite through that window. We know all too well what can happen when two teenagers (especially of the opposite sex) spend time in a bedroom alone. The other thing to consider is how easily children can sneak in and out of that window themselves. Your child's bedroom window is a perfect tool for the devil to use when he entices her to rebel against your curfew.

To protect your child, be on the alert for sounds near her bedroom window. If she's on the second floor, remove any structure that could be used to support someone. You might even want to consider something we did at our house: We installed a chime system that sounds whenever a window in the house is opened. If you have an alarm system in the house, a similar device can be added. Be sure to check regularly to ensure that the system is working properly. Also, every now and then walk outside the window and look for signs of traffic or activity, whether it be stools or chairs, disturbed landscape, damage to the window frame, or things that might have fallen from someone's pocket.

RULE—Under no circumstance can anyone pass through a bedroom window.

DISCIPLINE—Wild child lockdown: Room or house "arrest" for a specific period of time.

WILD PARENT ALTERNATIVE—Place security bars on the child's window.

2. Car Access

Without a doubt, the most exciting part of being a teenager, for me, was driving around with my friends. When my friend Mike got a car in our junior year of high school, he became DA MAN. Being in his car and driving around gave us freedom like nothing else. We could go where we wanted, when we wanted, and do whatever we wanted. And let me tell you, we took full advantage of our freedom. Unfortunately, as far as my parents were concerned, that spelled trouble. When I rode in Mike's car, they had no idea where I would end up or how I would get there. There are countless miles of roads out there, and as teenagers, we wanted to explore them all.

How much access to a car does your child have? Does she get your car whenever you're not using it? Rarely does a young person absolutely need a car. Also, keep in mind that your car is critical to your making a living and providing for your family. But in the minds of teenagers, a car is a fast and powerful toy that makes them popular. Their reasons for using the car will never be the whole truth and nothing but the truth. They want to be free to do all kinds of things, whether it be smoking, yelling and screaming, or going fast, without any restrictions.

Instead of feeling obligated to let your child use the car, turn it into one of your strongest sources of leverage. If she wants access to the car, require better grades, better behavior at home, better whatever. For all of these "betters," set specific guidelines about what is expected when she uses your car or rides in friends' cars: e.g., no smoking, no speeding, no riding without a seat belt. If the insurance coverage is in your name, and there's a lawsuit, it will be filed against you. You can also make a rule that your child cannot be alone in a car with someone of the opposite sex. You may even need to restrict certain friends from the car. Let that friend know why you don't want him or her in the car. It will carry more weight and may end up having a positive effect on that person.

Always check the mileage before and after your child uses

the car. Hold her accountable for where she goes, and keep an extra key. That's what Wally did to avoid living in fear about whether his daughter was being responsible with the car. For instance, one time she asked for the car and said she was going to the movies. He later drove to the parking lot of the theater and with his extra key opened the door to check the mileage and gas used. Upon her return, he checked it again.

You should also regularly check the glove compartment, ashtray, and under the seats for evidence of foul play, such as unusual smells. If you find something suspicious, accept no excuse that the evidence belongs to a friend. First Corinthians 15: 33 tells us, "Do not be deceived: 'Evil company corrupts good habits.' " So if your child is with someone in your car who is doing something you have forbidden, it will soon become the habit of your child.

Of course, all of this can be challenging, but cars can also create a great opportunity. Teach your child how to budget her money in order to pay for gas and fix any problems that arise from her use of the car. Washing the car or working on it together will also help strengthen your relationship with your child.

RULES—Before your child leaves with the car, confirm the odometer reading and gas level; know about any dings, dents, or scratches; and confirm the child's destination and expected time of return. Always have an extra key at your disposal. Require that everyone in the car wear a seat belt. Check the car for suspicious contents or smells upon its return.

DISCIPLINE—Deny car access to your child or certain friends for a specific period of time.

WILD PARENT ALTERNATIVES—Require that the child pay for the increase on the car insurance premium. Send him or her to prom in a yellow cab.

3. Music

After not seeing my nephew for about three years, I could hardly believe how he had changed. He had grown from an innocent ten-year-old to a very independent, wannabe grown-up thirteen-year-old. As the next Michael Jordan, he is now into picking out his own designer clothes and thinks he is more cool than I am. (Just kidding.) But probably the scariest thing about him was the music he was listening to: gangsta rap. He walked around listening to and singing about killing people, making money, and disrespecting women. I could see this attitude come out in what he called "playing around." It was obvious that the music was not having a positive effect on him. Unfortunately, he lives with his dad rather than my sister, who is very sensitive to the problem.

Satan has one thing in mind: to destroy your child. And he will do whatever is necessary and convenient to do so. Music is one of his most effective weapons. It will influence your child's beliefs and behavior, including who she hangs out with. The destructive messages in gangsta rap are common in rock, ska, punk, metal, and other kinds of music. They are only packaged differently.

The best way to check out your child's music is to listen to the lyrics of all the songs and screen them for content. If you have trouble picking out the words, many CDs include lyrics on the liner notes. Deciding what music is wrong is very simple. If it is dishonoring to God or if it talks about something you don't want your child doing or thinking about, it is the wrong music.

Try not to come across as judgmental. Teenagers take their music very personally and look up to their favorite artists, so keep your comments on a friendly basis, if possible. Because children don't always realize the destructive messages behind some music, ask your child to research her favorite artists—including their musical reputation, songs they've written and sung, even their existing arrest records—and report back to you. Let the facts speak for themselves. And then, if necessary, keep your child from pumping the wrong music into her head by prohibiting objectionable CDs in the house and car.

RULES—Approve all music before your child brings it home. Read all lyrics and require him or her to do an extensive background check and write a report on favorite musicians.

DISCIPLINE—Confiscate all music-playing equipment, including CD players, stereos, and radios, until further notice. Require your child to write a report on the true meaning of praise and worship music as well as the use of music in the Bible.

WILD PARENT ALTERNATIVE—Require the wild child to listen only to classical music for an hour each day.

4. School Performance

One day I came home and heard the following message on our answering machine: "Miles, I have your daughter, Kelly, here in my office, and she is in a bit of trouble. She was caught writing on the lockers, 'Danny and Kelly forever.' "

My first thought was *How could I have missed this?* Then I began to wonder if Danny preferred cremation or a traditional burial. As soon as these thoughts ran through my mind, the silence on the machine ended with the principal's saying,

"April fool!" Then I began thinking about the principal's burial preference!

I have to admit the phone call was kind of funny. And from that point on, I have continually asked school officials, "Has a boy named Danny enrolled yet? If not, is there someone here whose name starts with a *D*?" In reality, that phone call has led to my being in close contact with the principal and my monitoring my daughter's life at school. He knows that every time he sees me, I am going to ask how Kelly is doing. I want to avoid any surprises.

Many school counselors say their biggest frustration is the lack of parent involvement, so get involved in your child's education. Make a point of knowing his or her teachers and their expectations, when report cards are issued, and when homework is due and exams are given. Establish an agreement with teachers that you will see and sign all graded papers. The famous words "I already did my homework" mean nothing. Set regular homework and reading times in the home, and help or supervise your child when necessary. Also, find someone in the school who will go that extra mile for you and let you know if your child is missing classes or is tardy. Usually teachers and administrators are in the school business because they love kids and want to help your child. Yes, every now and then you might run into a staff member who is simply putting in his or her time and does not want to go the extra mile or do a good job, but this is not the norm. Don't wait until your child has serious problems before you set up these support systems.

Statistics show that students who do poorly are more apt to do drugs and be sexually active. Since personal achievement is closely tied to self-esteem and self-image, it is important that children succeed in school and feel good about themselves. If they are not successful at schoolwork, they will gravitate to something else they can succeed in, which often means trouble.

RULES—Write down and post scheduled study and reading times as well as grade expectations. Require your child to provide you with his or her class schedule.

DISCIPLINE—Increase study time and limit, if not prohibit, television use, time with friends, and participation in extra-curricular activities.

WILD PARENT ALTERNATIVE—For one week, require the wild child to go to school wearing a pocket protector with ten colored pens and pencils in it, high-water pants, argyle socks, and loafers.

5. Friends

Laurie was having trouble with her son coming home late—and drunk. She did not understand how he was getting the alcohol, since he was only fifteen. After interrogating her son, however, it became evident that he was going to parties at his friend's home, where alcohol was served.

Like you, I want to be the best parent I can be. Unfortunately, our children's friends and even their parents may not share our concerns and, in fact, can be bad influences. Here are some important things to know about your child's friends and their parents:

- Where do they live?
- Have they ever been in trouble before, and if so, what kind?
- What are their phone numbers?
- What are their parents' names? (If they are divorced, get information for both parents.)
- What are the parents' views on alcohol and drugs? Un-

supervised parties? Dating, curfews, discipline, smoking, premarital sex?

I challenged a parent to get this information, and she expressed her fear of not being able to ask these questions without offending another parent or appearing critical. She had a good point, so here are a few tips to keep in mind when you address these issues.

First, if possible, try to get to know the parents of your child's friends before a specific incident makes it necessary. Set up a meeting in a friendly atmosphere to discuss issues concerning *your* child, not problems you have with the friend. Your desire is to be the best parent possible, and one way to do this is to get ideas from other parents. Make them feel as though you are trying to learn from them. Hopefully, in the process, they will be open to learning something from you, which is especially important if a disagreement arises. The goal shouldn't be to change their views on anything but simply to learn about those views so you can act accordingly. Because your child will be spending time with their child, it is important to try to maintain open lines of communication, even if there is a difference of opinion. When they do express an opinion that opposes yours, try to gently steer them toward considering your point of view. If you sense there is no bending, don't argue—it won't change anything. Instead, move on to another subject, and then later decide how critical the differences are.

Take notes during the meeting. This will not only help you remember what was said but it will also let the others know you are serious about your child and her friends and their parents. It will also give the other parents a higher sense of accountability when your child is around them.

In the end, if your child's friend and his or her parents are a bad influence, do not be afraid to forbid your child from seeing them. She'll probably get angry, but she'll soon find another friend.

RULE—Interview and approve all of your child's friends and their parents.

DISCIPLINE—If your child still hangs out with a friend you have forbidden, limit your child's privileges.

WILD PARENT ALTERNATIVE—Visit the homes of prohibited friends and let them and their parents know about your request for no further contact.

LIE #19: Your child deserves a hangout of his or her own that is off limits to parents.

Does your child have a favorite hangout or two? Have you ever been there and checked it out? Or has she made it known that you aren't welcome there? Perhaps you've even felt she deserves a hangout of her own. This is exactly what the devil wants you to think. But your child's world is your world, too. There is nothing that pertains to them and their life that is not your business to know.

6. Where to Hang Out?

When I was a preteen I loved going to a park in my neighborhood to play basketball. In addition to basketball courts, there were play areas for little kids. Ironically, at night the swings and jungle gyms became a place for drug deals and gambling. Even though I was pretty young, I knew enough to stay away from that place and the older kids and adults who hung out there. I didn't want to fall into that kind of activity, even a few years later when some of my peers frequented the area.

One day when I was at the park, I heard some sudden screaming. I looked up and saw people running everywhere. Then I saw the father of one of my friends chasing a man up some stairs. He stopped just above the area where the guys would shoot dice and began shouting at another friend of mine. I stood frozen the entire time, watching in disbelief.

It turned out that the parent was chasing a guy who had been harassing his son to buy drugs. The father invaded the dealers' turf and made it clear that he wasn't going to let them ruin his son's life. After that no one ever harassed his son again.

I don't advocate running through a park shouting and causing a scene, but I do encourage you to make your presence known wherever your child hangs out. Young people need to know that there is absolutely no place their parents won't go or show up unannounced. Believe me, it will make a difference. Once your child sees you on her turf, that area will lose its luster for mischief. When you do check out your child's hangouts, it's smart to go with another parent and just walk around, talking with other kids to get a feel for what goes on there.

As you investigate your child's hangouts, find out if there is any supervision. Is there opportunity for drugs or alcohol to be used? Is it known for drug selling or gang activity, or is it a high crime area? Your local police department can answer most of your questions about neighborhood spots.

Talk to your child about her hangouts and their potential for danger. Ask detailed questions about who hangs out there and what goes on. The Bible says there is foolishness bound up in the heart of a child and that the mouth speaks from the overflow of the heart (Proverbs 22:15a; Matthew 12:34), so question everything she says. Questioning what children say does not mean they are liars, but it does mean a lot of foolishness is spoken, and we need to pray for discernment. If you don't feel good about a hangout, forbid your child from it.

When it comes to keeping a wild child out of trouble, it also helps to keep a "leash" on her. This can be accomplished by requiring your child to check in by phone every hour on the hour. Forgetting or not being near a phone is no excuse for not checking in. You might even want to purchase a cell phone or beeper for your child. She must not feel that she has the freedom to be alone and at the same time not be reachable or "yankable." Set up clear guidelines for communication. And don't accept excuses that the phone "accidentally" got turned off or the battery ran out. She must learn that excuses don't cut it in the real world.

RULE—Investigate and approve all hangout spots of the wild child.

DISCIPLINE—Restrict your child's time with friends or other privileges.

WILD PARENT ALTERNATIVE—If you are the mother, visit the hangout spot wearing hair rollers and a bathrobe—and hold hands with your child.

7. Bedroom Access

One day as a teenager, when no one was home, I brought a girlfriend into my bedroom to do what teenagers do in a bedroom when no one is home. While . . . should I say, I was relaxing in the comfort of my own bed, I heard a sound. Before I could react, I was living my worst nightmare. The door flung open, and there was my mom standing in the doorway! Needless to say, I was busted and could not be trusted any longer. Do you think that because it was my room a knock was in order? Well, busting into my room without any notice or warning was not only my mother's right, it was also her responsibility.

When was the last time you walked into your child's bedroom? Yes, there are times when children deserve privacy and a knock is appropriate, but in the long run, you have the right—under circumstances that you deem necessary—to walk right on in. The question is, do you have the courage? If your child were in her room and obviously in trouble—screaming, choking, or moaning—you wouldn't ask permission to enter the room. Think about it. You should feel the same urgency if you think that she might be doing something in her bedroom that is destructive to herself.

Do you have access to your child's bedroom? Do you know what she keeps in there? Can you enter any time you feel like it, or does she keep the door closed, playing loud music perhaps to keep you out?

Cindy was suspicious about her son's situation. She wanted so badly to go into his room and look around. The day she drew up the courage to walk in, she found herself locked out. Her own son's bedroom was literally off limits to her.

This is totally unacceptable. As I said, everyone has a right to some degree of privacy, but to be locked out of your own child's bedroom is something altogether different.

Your child may lock her door, claiming that she doesn't want her brother or sister to come in and get into her things. This is a valid point, but you must let your child know that nothing in the home is off limits to you as her parent, and require that you have a key to the bedroom. You also need to alert her siblings that they should not enter her room without her permission. A family must be built on mutual love and trust.

Carol and I went to high school together, but we were not close until I graduated from college. We'd hang out together, but only as friends. At her house, her father made it very clear that no one of the male species was allowed upstairs, where her bedroom was, not even cousins or Grandpa. When Carol told me about the "No boys upstairs" policy, I thought I would have some fun with it. One evening while talking with her parents, I announced that I was going upstairs. Immediately her father yelled, "Oh no, you're not!" I replied, "Why not? I was up there last week"—followed by a laugh to let him know that I was only joking!

RULE—No one of the opposite sex is allowed in the wild child's bedroom at any time, under any circumstance.

DISCIPLINE—Prohibit both male and female friends from the house for a period of time. Prohibit your child from associating with the friend who was found in her room.

WILD PARENT ALTERNATIVE—Remove the child's bedroom door from its hinges and force her to sleep on the couch for a period of time.

8. Job Performance

Having a job is great for helping kids to develop self-esteem, independence, responsibility, and discipline. Of course, this only happens if your child performs well on the job. That's why you should monitor and support your child's efforts at work, just as you do her efforts at school.

Get to know her boss or supervisor, their expectations, the anticipated work hours. Use this time to teach your child about good work ethics and being a good employee. Be involved in her development as an employee. Visit her workplace and talk with a supervisor about how she's doing. Is she on time? Is she learning to become a better employee? Is there an opportunity for advancement? Are there additional training and educational requirements? If so, do what you can to encourage your child. Provide certain privileges or freedoms around the house. Let her know what she is capable of when she puts her mind to something. The more positive dots you can connect between doing well in a job and at school and behavioral issues, the better the picture will look in the end. If your child is performing poorly, make it a requirement that she find a job that she can enjoy and excel in. It will make a world of difference in her life (and yours).

Earning money and being responsible for certain expenses is valuable preparation for the real world. Teenagers who are able to work—especially rebellious, uncooperative ones—should have to pay for some things themselves. However, working does not make a teenager totally independent of parental control and authority. Depending on the situation, you might want to collect your child's paycheck and withhold money for a percentage of food and rent expenses. Controlling your child's paycheck can also be used as leverage for satisfactory behavior around the house.

RULE—Require the wild child to complete a wild parent job assessment form (see page 99).

DISCIPLINE—Fine the wild child for pain and suffering by garnishing his or her wages for rent, heat, transportation, and light bills.

WILD PARENT ALTERNATIVE—Show up at your child's job unannounced and hang out for an undisclosed period of time.

9. Church Involvement

The million-dollar question for most parents is should I force my child to go to church?

It is vitally important and biblically essential for children to adopt their own faith in God. You cannot force someone to love God; it is only by the Holy Spirit that someone can say Jesus is Lord. It is a work of God. What you can do, however, is expose your child to the Word of God and to Christian influences that will give her a good opportunity to get to know God, so that she will be more apt to choose Him when the time is right for her.

Since 1996 I have been conducting Miles Ahead Crusades around the country for youth. These free events are designed to attract, entertain, and then confront non-Christian kids with the Gospel message. The crusades very much resemble Christian concerts, except they conclude with a clear and powerful Gospel message. Kids can come and have fun as they experience as good a Christian concert as they would ever pay for. Nonbelievers mix with Christian kids and are exposed to a cool and contemporary version of the Christian faith.

For your child, find a church that is youth-oriented and puts on fun ministry events for teenagers. Many churches organize events such as youth camps and one-day retreats. Ask kids who are involved in the church's activities if they would invite your child. "Sell" your child on the fun, and hopefully it will lead to God's being part of her life. No matter what, the church's fun is better than the world's fun. In addition, give your child CDs and books that reflect your Christian values.

It would be great if our children would just fall in love with God, but don't despise slow or small beginnings. Above all, pray for your child's faith. If you do so, something as simple as a church camp or Christian CD may spark a light in her heart.

RULE—Require the wild child to participate in a weekly family Bible study and write a short report on what was learned. He or she should also attend church when you do. Parents, pray with and for your child daily.

DISCIPLINE—Impose restrictions on the child's freedoms.

WILD PARENT ALTERNATIVE—Become a missionary and move your family to a remote South American country to do ministry.

Review Questions

1. Appropriate biblical rules are necessary for what two reasons?
2. What interests or desires does your child have that could be used for leverage when enforcing a rule?
3. Of the nine vulnerable areas presented in this chapter, which two or three create the most problems in your family?
4. What rules or guidelines will address these problem areas?

Chemo-Prayers Time

Lie #17: Rules in the home will take the fun out of your relationship with your child.

Dear Lord, thank you for your Word. Without rules in my life, I would be a mess. Proverbs 12:1 says, "Whoever loves instruction loves knowledge, but he who hates correction is stupid." I realize this applies to both the person who disdains giving correction and the person who doesn't want to receive it.

I thank you for the guidelines and rules in your Word. Satan must be a fool to think that this does not apply to the life of the wild child. Lord, I pray Proverbs 15:5 on the life of my child: "A fool despises his father's instruction, but he who receives correction is prudent." I pray that I can give instruction and establish biblical rules according to my child's needs.

Lie #18: Parents don't have a right to know and control everything that happens in the home.

Dear Lord, I thank you for giving my child to me. You say in Psalm 127:3 that children are a heritage and reward from you. You also tell me in Proverbs 22:6: "Train a child in the way he should go, and when he is old he will not depart from it." These verses clearly tell me that I have a responsibility to raise my child correctly. Please grant me the courage to do whatever is necessary to fulfill my responsibility as a parent.

Lie #19: Your child deserves a hangout of his or her own that is off limits to parents.

Dear Lord, thank you for your Word. I realize that children left to themselves will bring shame on their families and parents. I realize that Satan loves to do his evil work in darkness and isolation. John 3:20–21 says, "For everyone practicing evil hates the light and does not come to the light, lest his deeds should be exposed. But he who does the truth comes to the light, that his deeds may be clearly seen, that they have been done in God."

I pray that in a loving and godly way I will be able to serve notice to my child and family that no place is off limits to the light. May I be the conduit for that light in the life of my child.

Wild Parent Job Assessment

This assessment is designed to help the wild child think through some of the issues related to successful, long-term employment. By having your teenager answer the following questions, you will help encourage him or her to become a faithful and dependable worker.

COMPLETE THE FOLLOWING QUESTIONS:

1. What is the title of your job?
2. What is the purpose of your job?
3. What top three duties must you master in order to do a good job?
4. To whom are you accountable?
5. Provide a weekly or monthly work schedule: times and days required to be at work.
6. What is the pay scale for your position?
7. What is your weekly and monthly take-home pay?
8. What are your plans for spending the money? Provide a budget.
9. At your present job level, what is required to get a raise?
10. How much could that raise be?
11. What position is just above yours, and what are that person's responsibilites?
12. What is required to advance in the company? (education level, experience, certain skills, etc.)
13. What's your ideal job?

Chapter Five

WILD TRAINING: CHEMO-DISCIPLINE

ONCE A DIAGNOSIS OF CANCER is confirmed, doctors order a biopsy to get a more accurate picture of the extent and type of cancer they're facing. Proper treatment is then prescribed. If the cancer is confined to a specific place in the body, it is surgically removed or treated with radiation, which simply kills everything in its path.

As mentioned earlier, Caroline's first course of treatment involved removing the cancerous lump from her breast. This was considered a local treatment. Unfortunately, it did not solve Caroline's problem. The cancer had spread to other areas in her body, making a second type of treatment—systemic treatment—essential. Chemotherapy is considered systemic because cancer-killing drugs are injected into the bloodstream and travel throughout the body. Even though the drug attacks cancer cells, it also kills some healthy cells, which is why patients often get sick to their stomach, lose their hair, and also experience a weakened immune system, which puts them at risk for other illnesses. Chemotherapy, because of its effect on the entire body, can bring a person to the point of death. The trick is to give patients as much chemotherapy as they can handle without killing them.

Caroline's first chemotherapy treatment was nerve-racking. It only required a half-day at the hospital, but she was quickly convinced even more of its seriousness when they placed an IV into her arm and then brought in the medicine. The bag read: *"Danger, the chemicals contained in this package are lethal. . . ."* In other words, to save Caroline's life, they needed to inject chemicals that could potentially kill her.

Disciplining the wild child when he or she breaks a rule is an important element of treatment. It is the act of establishing and administering the bottom line. In other words, your child's inappropriate action must guarantee a certain loving, correcting reaction from you as a parent. Discipline won't kill your child, but it can and oftentimes does hurt. It may even be painful for you.

When deciding how you should respond to wild-child behavior, you must remember that this is a life-or-death situation. Treat any sign of rebellion as life-threatening. This is the best safeguard against rebellion becoming more serious. The devil wants your child for his own. Knowing the severity of the situation should make it easier for you to administer the necessary treatment.

Satan will tell you that discipline could kill your relationship with your child and that he will rebel even more and blame you for alienating him. But as the physician in this case, you must make the hard decision to administer the appropriate medicine. You must be willing to trust God with your child and allow Him to work in his heart as you treat him. It may even mean letting your child hit rock bottom—allow him to be arrested, spend time in jail, or live on the street.

With cancer, if the proper amount of treatment is not given, the patient will die. This is very important to keep in mind. Very often people go through a stage of denial when they find out they have cancer. They don't want to believe that it is serious and they could die. They seek other opinions, hoping someone will tell them what they want to hear. But when all is said and done, they usually give in to the fact that something needs to be done to save their life. As odd as it may seem, however, some cancer patients remain in denial so long about their need for treatment that they die before receiving it.

If you think your wild child's problems will disappear if ignored, you are deceived. John 10:10 says, "The thief does not come except to steal, and to kill, and to destroy. I have come that they may have life, and that they may have it more abundantly." Satan is the ultimate destroyer and murderer. His number one goal is to destroy the life of your child. Your child might not physically die before his normal life expectancy, but his dreams and hopes will die. He will lose his drive to dream and pursue an abundant life through Jesus. He will lose all hope of being restored to God and to your family.

LIE #20: Children know right from wrong and don't need discipline.

You have a biblical responsibility to discipline your children. Proverbs 22:15 says, "Foolishness is bound up in the heart of a child; The rod of correction will drive it far from him." Children are going to do foolish things, and only by discipline and correction will they learn the right way.

In addition, if you do not discipline your child and represent discipline and righteousness in the home, sooner or later someone else will. School officials, employers, or other kids on the street will end up dealing with his wild and out-of-control attitude. If none of these people do it, you can always count on the police to administer impartial discipline.

Proverbs 29:15 says, "The rod and rebuke give wisdom, but a child left to himself brings shame to his mother." If you do nothing about your wild child, the shame will come back on you. It will be shameful to go into the juvenile detention center to visit him. It will be shameful when people ask, "How is your son?" It will be shameful when he gets caught stealing and you have to leave work to bring him home. There is no question that children can bring shame on the best of parents, but if it happens because a parent is ignoring his or her child's behavior, it is especially painful.

The lack of discipline and correction in a family is the devil's desire. He would love children never to learn to submit to authority. A child who has no sense of self-control or ability to live within the boundary of rules best serves the devil's purposes. Satan loves a child who is willing to push the limits of what he is allowed to do, to be defiant in the face of elders. This is the classic trait of a wild child.

Satan might have turned you against hard discipline when your child was younger. You vowed never to spank him or do anything that would create a bad memory. Instead, you spent his childhood negotiating with him about punishment. You gave him discipline options from which to choose, or you gave him repeated chances to prove that he could do the right thing. In the process, the only thing he probably learned was how far he could push you or how much he could get away with before you would actually do something.

Some parents let children have their way, thinking they will grow out of their childish, rebellious ways. But it never happens. They become teenagers who act as selfish and childish as toddlers. The only problem is, now their toys are cars, furniture, and the hearts of their family. I have heard these parents in the stores: "Johnny . . . Johnny, I'm not going to tell you again." Meanwhile, Johnny knows that he has about nine more "Johnnies" before he really needs to get it together. Johnny needs to experience the wrath of Mom or Dad. But the question is, does that wrath even exist?

Satan will also try to fool you into thinking that the threat of discipline or weak enforcement of discipline is the same as effective discipline. In other words, you threaten discipline but you never follow through. You might find yourself saying, "I will let you go this time, but next time will be different." I am not saying that you should never let a child off the hook, but children are quick learners. Before you know it, they've learned how to manipulate you to escape punishment. In addition, if you do finally impose punishment, you will be made to feel like the bad guy, making it even harder the next time.

Some parents feel handcuffed or limited on how far they can and should hand out discipline. When it comes to dealing with the wild child, you must realize that there is no limit to how far they will go or how far Satan will push them in their rebellion. Therefore, you need to be prepared to throw all your limits out the window. No holds are barred when it comes to doling out appropriate, loving discipline. Remember, lives are at stake. Not only the life of your wild child but also the lives of everyone else in the family.

LIE #21: If I start disciplining my child, he will rebel even more and I will lose him.

Satan will fill you with the fear of losing your child. He will tell you that discipline will anger your child. Let's think about that for a second. What would your child really do if he were mad? Yell at you? Get angry and lock himself in his room? Not talk to you? When this happens, you need to remember the reason behind the discipline—to administer treatment to save your child's life.

Some kids will threaten to run away or harm themselves in some other way. They are counting on their parents to love them so much that they back down. If this happens in your family, there will come a time when you need to call your child's bluff. Unless your child is suicidal, you need to be willing to let him follow through on his threat for two reasons. First, you must prove that you are serious about what you believe to be right. After all, if he is serious about doing something wrong—serious enough to back it up with action—you need to be at least as serious about doing what is right. The second reason is that your child needs to realize for himself that Satan is a two-time liar.

The only reason your child is threatening to run away or harm himself is because Satan has told him that you will back down. And the first way you can expose Satan as a liar is to stand firm. The second way to prove to your child that Satan is the Father of Lies is to let your child go. He has been told that your rules and regulations stand in the way of freedom, fun, and excitement. If he goes out on his own, he will be free indeed. Well, you and I know that Satan is only deceiving your child. If he leaves the house, there is no way it will be good for him long term. Eventually your child's sin will bring him to his knees. He'll realize that Satan lied about the fun and excitement.

This is where your faith in the Lord will come in. You will have to be in constant prayer that God spares your child. But isn't He doing this already? Isn't He keeping your child even as you read this book? You and I know that our kids could have been long gone by now if it had not been for the saving grace of our Lord.

Trust God with these impossible problems. Let your child go, let your fears go, and take back control of your home and your family. After all, if a child really wants to do something crazy, we can't stop him.

Ricky's son Larry was addicted to crack and had been stealing from the family for some time. Finally, his father kicked him out of the house. Larry's habit got worse—so bad that he began to sell his body to other men. One night Larry called home and said he needed money for food. When Ricky met him, Larry told his dad all about his lifestyle. Larry asked to come home, so he would not have to prostitute himself. As horrible as this was for Ricky to hear, he had to make a decision: take his son back or continue to call his bluff.

He decided to leave him on the street.

Why? Ricky knew Larry wasn't ready to change, and he wanted to protect the rest of the family from continued pain. He also wanted Larry to know he was serious about Larry's need to change. Ultimately, Ricky's decision gave Satan the chance to prove to Larry that he did not have Larry's best interest in mind! In the story of the prodigal, Luke 15:17 says, "But when he came to himself, he said, 'How many of my father's hired servants have bread enough to spare, and I perish with hunger!' "

LIE #22: A little dose of discipline now and then will be enough to straighten out a wild child.

One of the keys to effective cancer treatment is that it must be consistent until the cancer is gone. This same principle applies to disciplining your child. You cannot expect to bring about change in your child's life if you are inconsistent about discipline.

Discipline is hard work because it involves figuring out appropriate and meaningful consequences. However, it should be administered calmly with this thought in mind: *What is best for my child?*

Continually examine your motivation for discipline. Sometimes we can get so worn down dealing with problems that we'll do almost anything just to have some peace for ourselves. However, a doctor should never treat his patient for his own sake but only to improve or to save the life of the patient. Keeping the child's interests first will also help you to keep a long-term perspective with regard to your discipline practices. *Focus your discipline and guidance on teaching lasting lessons rather than stopping misbehavior every now and then.*

As you know all too well, parenting a wild child is difficult. Countless decisions must be made for situations that crop up daily. Beyond discipline issues, it is work finding the right people to help your child, the right church for him, and hopefully the right friends. It is work keeping a child away from the wrong friends and hangouts. But the work is necessary and vital to your child's survival. You must be prayerful about doing the things that will help your child not only be delivered from his pain and destructive behavior but also to begin to live a productive life.

LIE #23: If my child makes me mad, he deserves whatever trouble comes his way.

One way of monitoring your discipline is to remember never to discipline out of anger. This never brings about a positive attitude or behavior change. Anger-based discipline is usually aimed at returning the pain a parent has felt: *You hurt me, and now I am going to hurt you back.* Hurting your child in return for his behavior is not only unbiblical but it is also counterproductive.

During a recent outreach to an inner-city neighborhood, we handed out over twenty-five hundred of my football cards to all the kids who showed up. While I sat and signed them, I noticed a boy about three years old waiting for a second autograph, but his mother was not so patient. She kept calling to him to get out of the line. Finally she walked over and pulled on his jacket until he fell over. He started to cry, but she walked away, leaving him on the floor. A twelve-year-old girl stood nearby, holding her six-month-old brother. I looked at the girl and said, "Don't ever do that to a little kid." She nodded her head in agreement.

If you are dealing with a teenager this way—allowing your emotions, frustrations, and anger to lash out—you will not accomplish anything worthwhile. Never discipline your child in a way that will make you feel better, appear in control, or look good in front of your friends. When you have been embarrassed by your child or been shown disrespect in front of other people, the temptation is to react in anger. You might feel like you need to reestablish your authority by yelling louder or punishing harshly to show who is the boss. But if harsh discipline really worked, your child wouldn't be doing these things over and over again.

The wild child has been led to believe that your emotions can be manipulated. Satan has told him that your judgment is not clear when you are angry, and this is true. Therefore, you must decide to be methodical and thoughtful about your discipline. When things happen, try not to react out of anger or surprise. Don't live on the edge of your seat, constantly saying to yourself, *I don't know what I am going to do!* Figure it out ahead of time. The first thing you should do is pray. When Job realized that he had lost everything he ever owned, including his children, what did he do? "Then Job arose and tore his robe and shaved his head, and he fell to the ground and worshiped. And he said: 'Naked I came from my mother's womb, and naked shall I return there. The Lord gave, and the Lord has taken away; blessed be the name of the Lord'" (Job 1:20–22).

In all of this, Job did not sin or charge God with wrong. He did not react like a crazed man and shout, "No, no, no, this can't be!" He did not yell and scream at God.

Set up a cooling-off rule as one of the basic guidelines that govern your family life. Following unacceptable behavior, your child should go to his room until he cools off and gets himself together, and until you can make a decision about what to do.

I should point out that criticizing your child has the same negative effect as anger-based discipline. Rather than bringing about a positive change, it can embitter your child. Don't ever use truth like a stick and beat your child with it. This is counterproductive. It is very important to speak the truth, but in a way that is beneficial. Ephesians 4:15 says, "[And we,] in speaking the truth in love, may grow up in all things into Him who is the head—Christ."

Sometimes we think pointing out someone's wrongs will make the person stop doing it. This is not always the case, especially with the wild child. They do not always misbehave intentionally or to hurt you. Sometimes they cannot help what they are doing. They are out of control, and need help. Think about it: Jesus went all the way to the cross to save us from our sins. He did not simply yell from heaven, "Hey, you guys, will you stop that sinning down there and begin obeying me?" Neither did he yell, "Start praying, and everything will be all right!" No! He came down here and modeled for us what we need to do. He gave us His Word as counsel. He suffered the ultimate pain and suffering: death on a cruel cross. Not only did He come down and die, but he also explained some things before His death: how we need to live, what is expected of us, and how we can get the power to do what is expected of us. Then He promised to send a Helper. John 14:26 says, "But the Helper, the Holy Spirit, whom the Father will send in My name, He will teach you all things, and bring to your remembrance all things that I said to you."

Telling your child what he is doing wrong is not going to make him stop. Simply letting him know his behavior bothers you will not force him to do differently. But discussing it with him is another story. Start the conversation with something like "I don't know if you realize this, but when you don't call when you are going to be late, it really bothers me, because . . ." Unfortunately, this doesn't *always* work, because some kids are so caught up in their own pleasure and addictions that they can't care about anyone except themselves. If your child doesn't care about what you think, he won't be as inclined to listen to what you have to say, and he won't be as concerned about respecting your rules.

Satan is going to do everything in his power to destroy you and your family, including attacking your self-confidence and sense of self-worth. There will be times when you will feel disrespected, hurt, and a failure as a parent. Your own child may even attack you verbally. Again, this is where prayer becomes your strongest ally. Through prayer, God will reassure you that your worth in Him can never be damaged or destroyed.

These feelings of low self-worth, if not acknowledged, will affect how you discipline and cause you to actually react counterproductively. Your anger toward your child could represent your own pain—your own frustrations about life and your feelings of failure as a parent. Satan is getting the best of you if he can get you to take out that frustration on your child. Don't underestimate the power of the devil to play with your mind and emotions.

Effective Discipline Must Be Decisive

My sister, Margaret, has a son and a daughter. She is a good mom and is very committed to her children. Mikey is literally a genius. He has a great desire to read, and we often laugh at his out-of-this-world ability to learn facts. Leah, my sister's eleven-year-old, is also very intelligent, but she can sometimes be a challenge. One day Margaret told Leah to clean her room. Leah ran upstairs, slammed her door, and fell asleep without cleaning her room!

Leah's actions violated several family rules. First, when you are told to do something, like clean your room, you do it—end of story. Second, storming upstairs and slamming a bedroom door is not acceptable.

After a while Margaret went upstairs and discovered a third violation: Leah's door was locked. She asked Leah about it, who explained from inside her room that the door was stuck and must have locked itself. Margaret couldn't believe her ears, so she asked again, "Did you lock this door?" Leah persisted in her denial. Well, after going back and forth, my sister became frustrated and hurt by her daughter's lie and gave up.

When Leah's dad came home, Margaret told him what Leah had done. Mike didn't say a word, but what he did spoke volumes. He went to the basement, strapped on his utility belt, and headed upstairs. My sister could only wonder what her husband was up to.

First, she heard a drill buzzing. In a few minutes, Mike came walking down the stairs with Leah's bedroom door. I never really liked Mike (just kidding), but I must say that now he is my hero. I think his response was the most amazing display of a parent letting his child know: "You are nowhere near being in control, and there is nothing I won't do to let you know that."

What are you willing to do to put your child in his rightful place? How much chemotherapy are you willing to administer? How much discomfort are you willing to put your child through? The maximum amount of chemotherapy that he can tolerate? Or a slow and easy flow, risking his death in the process?

Think about what was going through Leah's mind when her father took that door off its hinges and walked down the stairs with it. Think about how her life was drastically changed in a moment, all because of a choice she made to disobey and disrespect her mother, and also because her father had the courage not to let her get away with it. I would have to say that was a decisive, educational moment.

Effective Discipline Must Be Clear

It is important to make family guidelines very clear. Children need to know and understand—though not necessarily agree with—what will happen if they break certain rules. It needs to be crystal clear that if they wake up in the morning and plan to get high, they will be punished if they get caught.

Remember, Satan has told the wild child that there will be no consequences for his actions. The devil has convinced him that he can be like God: know good and evil and be able to decide right from wrong on his own. However, as you know, the gospel truth is that the penalty for sin is death. That doesn't necessarily mean physical death, but it does mean the death of freedom in his home and the death of his relationships with the people who love him most.

One way these truths become clouded in a family is if the parents are hesitant to administer discipline. If children know or think they can get away with something, the consequences won't really be clear to them. They will begin to believe the lies of the Evil One. When my brother-in-law took the door off the hinges, he did not yell, scream, or threaten Leah; he simply acted decisively and with big-time clarity. His daughter will never again think about locking that door. As a matter of fact, I don't think she will be closing it for some time.

Effective Discipline Must Be Godly

Discipline should be godly, something God would want, because it will drive your child to obedience. It should not be done in anger or with resentment, but in love. Make sure your child understands that there is more to discipline than punishment for doing something wrong. There are character issues involved, too.

Be sensitive to what God is leading you to do. Ask Him for wisdom about each situation. Doing this will show your child that God is still in charge, that you are allowing God to administer the discipline through you. "Likewise you younger people, submit yourselves to your elders. Yes, all of you be submissive to one another, and be clothed with humility, for 'God resists the proud, but gives grace to the humble' " (1 Peter 5:5). This verse is clear that if you discipline proudly God will resist you, but if you act with humility, He will afford you more grace.

Effective Discipline Must Be Prayerful and Compassionate

Gary was anxious to hang out with his friends, so he hurried to mow the lawn. When his mother told him the lawn was unacceptable and he had to do it again, he slapped her. She returned the slap and sent him to his room. When Gary Senior came home, more words were exchanged, and his father proceeded to inflict a whupping that Gary would not forget.

This wasn't the first nor would it be the last confrontation between Gary and his parents, but it was a turning point. Although Gary Senior was angry about his son's actions, he took the matter to God in prayer. He was heartbroken that his relationship with his son had reached such a low point. Still, in every family there must be a line that cannot be crossed. Proverbs 19:18 says, "Chasten your son while there is hope, and do not set your heart on his destruction." In other words, you should not be out to punish but to train and admonish in the Lord. So when Gary threatened to move out, his dad tossed his luggage on the bed, looked him in the eye, and said, "Goodbye. You have to go, because I will not have anyone treat my wife that way ever again."

It was then that Gary Junior knew that he had messed up and needed to be punished. He realized that he was out of control. The Bible says that the heart knows its own bitterness and no one can share its joy (Proverbs 14:10). It may take a while, but hopefully one day your child will know that he has messed up and deserves to be disciplined.

Effective Discipline Must Have a Final Word: Yours

The most crucial part of discipline is that your word must be final. Once you rule on a situation, the ruling must stand

and follow-through must be complete. This is the hardest aspect of regaining parental control, because chances are you have been allowing rules to be broken or haven't been consistent about consequences.

There must be an ace card that you can play, one that will strike fear in your child's heart. For some this is physical punishment, but I am not talking about that. You must be able to identify how far you are willing to go, not only to save your child but the rest of family, which is being torn apart by the wild child. There must be a line that teenagers know never to cross unless they are already packed and ready to move out.

Ron and Teresa had a good relationship with their oldest boy, Lance. Ron says young Lance was a model kid who would do everything he was told the first time. When Lance was old enough, he started working for Ron in construction. But soon things were not right. Tools began disappearing from the shop; items from home were missing also. Ron realized then that his son was on drugs. Ron and Teresa tried to help Lance, but things got so bad that he started to bring down the entire family. They knew drastic measures were necessary. Ron and Teresa told Lance that if he came home high one more time, they were going to have him arrested and he would never live in their home again.

A short time later police came to their home and hand-cuffed Lance in front of his two brothers. He pleaded with Ron and Teresa, "Please, don't let them take me. Please, don't let them take me. I won't do it anymore." How many times have you heard your child say that? Ron and Teresa had heard one too many false promises. Isn't it ironic that the wild child becomes a master at making false promises? Does that give you a hint as to where the false promises are coming from? So many parents believe these promises. Believe me, a child cannot truly change without the Lord's help.

You can imagine the pain Lance's parents experienced that day, especially his mother. But there must come a time when a wild child's second chances run out. This is what effective discipline is all about. When Lance's "cancer" (drug use) had revealed itself, Ron and Teresa made a commitment to administer the necessary chemo-discipline. They knew that if they did not, death would result. Once you make a decision on discipline, you must follow through.

Putting your foot down is not only an opportunity to teach and train the wild child but it also has an impact on other children in the family. Lance's arrest hurt his parents, but it shocked his brothers. They know that their dad doesn't want to lose them to drugs and that he will administer a drug test on the spot.

Let me tell you, unless your other children are very young, they know what is going on with the wild child. They also have an opinion about what should be done, even though they may also be testing you to see how far they can push the behavior envelope. Parents who take a strong stand with a wild child find that they become bolder about disciplining their other children. They are quick to straighten things out when anyone else in the family becomes crooked.

You must discern when it is the right time to ease up on your stance. This is why prayer and unity in prayer are so important. After Lance got out of jail, there were times when Ron wanted his son to come home. Lance would send letters saying how much he missed the family and how he wanted to move back and work with his dad again. At first, Ron and Teresa's hearts would break over these letters, but after praying about what to do, they still felt coming home would not help Lance.

Whatever you do, don't second-guess yourself. Satan will bombard you with guilt over your decision about discipline only later to suggest more lenient alternatives. But the trap is realized when these alternatives backfire and Satan accuses you of being weak and indecisive. Listen to God, and He will guide you.

It has been three years since Lance's arrest. He is now completely recovered from his addictions and has a family, a job, and a new life in Louisiana. While taking Lance to the airport after a recent visit, Ron and Teresa asked him what finally turned him around. His response shocked but blessed them. He said it wasn't anything anyone had said to him. It was God. Their discipline had put their son in a place where God became his only—but most powerful—alternative.

Review Questions

1. Do you have firm discipline guidelines that everyone in the family is clear about?
2. What percentage of the time do you discipline out of anger?
3. Do you discipline out of personal convenience?
4. Have you kept your end of the disciplining bargain by sticking to your promises?

Chemo-Prayers Time
Lie #20: Children know right from wrong and don't need discipline.

Dear Lord, thank you for your Word. I know that my child cannot possibly judge right from wrong on his own. Proverbs 22:15 clearly says, "Foolishness is bound up in the heart of a child; The rod of correction will drive it far from him." I pray that I would keep this in mind when Satan tries to convince me that my child truly understands how to use sound judgment. I pray today for the wisdom to discern what lessons need to be taught through discipline.

Lie #21: If I start disciplining my child, he will rebel even more and I will lose him.

Dear Lord, thank you for your Word. I pray that instead of fearing the results of my discipline, I would do it out of obedience to you. Proverbs 3:12 says, "For whom the Lord loves He corrects, just as a father the son in whom he delights." This clearly means that discipline is a way of showing love to my child. It will keep my child out of trouble when he gets older. Please grant me the courage to obey your guidance.

Lie #22: A little dose of discipline now and then will be enough to straighten out a wild child.

Dear Lord, thank you for your Word. Lord, I know that I need to be consistent in my discipline. It needs to be both prompt and timely. I have hesitated and put if off in the past, and it has lost its effectiveness. Proverbs 13:24 says, "He who spares his rod hates his son, But he who loves him disciplines him promptly." Please grant me the courage to do what a loving parent is supposed to do.

Lie #23: If my child makes me mad, he deserves whatever trouble comes his way.

Dear Lord, thank you for your Word. Lord, I know that I often get mad at my child and want to inflict pain out of frustration. But Proverbs 19:18 says, "Chasten your son while there is hope, and do not set your heart on his destruction." Even though I need to discipline, please give me a compassionate heart so that I may discipline in order to train and admonish. Ephesians 6:4 says, "And you, fathers, do not provoke your children to wrath, but bring them up in the training and admonition of the Lord."

Chapter Six

WILD COMMUNICATION: TALK WITH ME!

ONE OF THE MOST IMPORTANT aspects of cancer treatment is conducting a series of tests throughout the process. In Caroline's case, blood tests helped the doctor measure tumor markers, which indicate the tumor level in her body. These tests were also used to monitor how well the body was responding to the dangerous but necessary chemotherapy. If test results were satisfactory, he would continue treatment as planned, and if not, adjustments would be made.

Caroline was subjected to countless needle pokes in her arms, back, and head. Blood tests provided endless information about her general health and the condition of her immune system. The number of cancer cells floating through her body was also measured. MRIs were done to search for tumors. Tests were conducted to check her respiratory function. Bone scans were ordered to see how her bones were holding up to chemotherapy. In addition, the doctors also monitored Caroline's mental and emotional health, especially as the treatments mounted.

The results of these tests were a way for her body to communicate with the doctors. In the same way, as your child goes through trials and tribulations, you must be in constant contact with her, monitoring how she is doing.

If our bodies were unable to "communicate," doctors wouldn't know if anything was going wrong or if medicine was working properly. In fact, the only time our bodies are unable to provide this type of information is when we die.

If communication stops, death follows. And that's Satan's goal. He wants you to cut the communication lines between you and your child, so that he can whisper even more lies into your child's ears. It is when we are isolated from sound and godly counsel that the devil's advice seems reasonable. It is when kids are alone and listening to the discouraging and depressing voice of the Evil One that they attempt suicide.

LIE #24: Talking *to* the wild child is the same as communicating *with* the wild child.

At times a strong relationship with the patient is not always a priority for doctors. They're often accused of being the "bottom line" type, only interested in data, test results, and prescriptions for cures. The only time these types of doctors talk to patients is to gather additional facts. Although this might be an overgeneralization, this style of communication is not an option for parents. Never view your conversations with your child as simply a means to get information.

Doctors have little need to develop long-term relationships with their patients (even though it would make the process more pleasant). When the treatment is over, doctors may never see the patient again. But this is not true with parents. Our kids are our kids forever, for better or for worse, for richer or for poorer, in sickness and in health. For you, there is a relationship to be developed. There is a life to be nurtured, not merely muzzled or tolerated. There is a child to be loved, not a patient to be saved.

Beyond gathering information, the art of communication is the successful exchange of thoughts, feelings, and ideas.

The most important communication goal for you as a parent is to help your child develop a relationship with you and with God. Successful communication takes effort, but it produces fruit like nothing else can. You don't need to talk with your child about everything all of the time, but you do need to do your part to make sure there is always an open line of communication between you two.

LIE #25: Even though my child and I don't talk much, we still have a strong relationship.

The average parent spends only seven minutes a day in meaningful, positive conversation with their children. From what kids tell me, this is probably accurate. They make comments like "My parents don't listen to me when I talk, anyway. They just nod their head and wait for me to go away."

I believe there is a direct correlation between the quality of communication between parent and child and the strength of that relationship. When I talk about your *relationship*, I am not addressing how much you and your child love each other but how well the two of you exchange thoughts, feelings, and ideas. We must be very intentional about beginning and sustaining conversations with our kids. The more we talk, the

more ideals and expectations can be exchanged, the more mis-
understandings can be cleared up, and the more love can flow
between us. On the other hand, when parents and children do
not communicate regularly, they are each left to guess about
what the other is thinking or feeling. If God never spoke to
you, how would you ever know what was expected of you? If
you never spoke to God, how could He ever know what you
wanted?

How well do you communicate with your child? What
percentage of your interactions takes the following forms?

- scolding or correcting
- teaching and training
- laughing with and enjoying your child
- discussing the day's events
- complaining about something he did or should have done

As you well know, creating opportunities for meaningful,
positive conversations with a wild child can be challenging. It
is important to try, however, because if everything you say is
negative, you will begin to represent bad news or a bad experience to your child. This will only reinforce the lies Satan is
telling her about you. If you want to be a godly influence, if
you want your child to be honest about her fears, failures, and
fantasies, you must pray for positive interaction.

Many parents feel they have nothing to talk with their kids
about. They think meaningful communication only occurs
during serious or educational conversation. But you must come
to believe that any kind of interaction with your child that is
not negative or counterproductive is a good thing. Conversation doesn't have to be full of lovey-dovey feelings and expres-
sions. In fact, just spending time with her will develop your
relationship and improve overall communication. A two-

minute chat about common, everyday things can turn into a more significant five- or ten-minute conversation.

One of the easiest ways to get the two-way connection going is to begin including your child in some of your daily activities, such as jogging, playing a game of pool, throwing a baseball, or cooking a meal. Challenge your child to a competition of some sort and include a little good-natured razzing. Watch a game on TV together or make a trip to the mall. Take your child to work; ask her to help you around the house and yard. Include her in your weekend outings and vacations. Just doing some kind of activity together will create its own conversation.

What do you talk with friends about? Why not have the same kinds of conversations with your child? Talk about current events or sports, trade jokes, and when you're both home in the evening, share stories from the day. Use the phone for short conversations. Sometimes my dad and I call each other up to five times a day, but many of those conversations last no longer than a minute. Typically, we are watching the same ball game on television, and I simply call him about a particular play. These aren't life-changing moments, but again, the goal is to create opportunities to connect.

Take this time to reinforce what you have in common with your child while also creating new memories. Get out old family pictures or home videos and refresh stories and memories of fun times. This is what my brothers and sisters do when we get together. We end up talking and laughing about the dumb things we did as children and funny incidents we remember from growing up. You may say to yourself, *We don't have any memories like that in our family*. Right now it might be difficult to remember better times, but if nothing else, your child will enjoy hearing stories about when she was a baby or a toddler.

Instead of being the "heavy" all the time and disciplining your child over and over again, make a point of saying something encouraging to her each day. Look for positives and let her know that you notice and appreciate them. Of course, to be a good encourager you need to know and understand what kind of encouragement she needs. What a perfect reason to try to understand what your child is going through, to try to see things from her point of view. The better you get at doing this, the more your child will see you as someone who is on her side and is looking out for her best interests.

In addition to giving the wild child counsel, request her advice about your situations or concerns. You might even ask how you should help another son or daughter. Of course, be careful not to share any private information, but most children appreciate helping to choose gifts or determining appropriate rewards for good behavior.

If your child is nearing driver's license age, you should be the one who teaches her how to drive. You can teach her how to save money to buy a car and how financing works. There is no wild child on the planet who wouldn't want more money and her own car. As I discussed in chapter 4, access to a car is a common danger area for teenagers, but as you teach your child life skills such as driving and money management, focus on the relationship you are building with your child rather than the risks that might lie ahead.

Successful communication goes far beyond the words exchanged. Nonverbal responses and messages are just as important. Try to pick up on your child's unspoken cues. For example, when she nods her head in agreement, does she really understand what you are saying or asking? Frustration builds when one person thinks everything is okay when it is not.

Not long ago I saw a documentary on Animal Planet, one of my favorite channels. It showed a veterinarian trying to save a lion that had eaten part of a leather strap. The operation, including how they sedated the lion, was fascinating. But what baffled me most was how veterinarians know what is wrong with sick animals. Obviously animals can't talk or communicate like humans can. They can't tell the doctor where it hurts. Consequently, veterinarians frequently have to touch possible pain points and interpret nonverbal responses.

As humans we have the great advantage of being able to talk. We can explain in detail where it hurts, how it hurts, and when it hurts. We can also express when things are going well. As parents it is critical for us to use our gift of communication in good times as well as bad. Too often we express ourselves only when there is pain, when we need to correct or discipline our children. Instead, we need to find out from them why they are hurting and how we can help.

When parents and teenagers don't talk with each other, it is often because of anger in the hearts of the children. A few years ago I filmed a video with a group of teenagers on the topic of anger and violence. As I prepared to make the video, I needed to develop a clear definition of and reason for anger. Here's what we came up with: People get angry when they don't get what they want or what they think they need.

When your child is angry with you, ask yourself, *Is there something she's not getting that she thinks she deserves?* It is important to know that we parents do not exist simply to satisfy all the wants of our children. Satan loves to tell kids that they deserve and need things they really don't need. But on the other hand, a growing teenager does have legitimate emotional, social, and psychological needs—even though she's not always able to articulate what they are.

Anger can also be a symptom of inner pain. If your child is angry, there is a good chance she is feeling hurt. Perhaps you have treated her unfairly or been too hard on her. Maybe you've shown disrespect toward her or been sarcastic with her. Only you can know if you have done these things. If you aren't sure, take your concerns to God in prayer; He will reveal to you what you may be doing to hurt your child. If you are causing hurt, it is going to require humility to not only change your attitude and ways but also to ask your child for forgiveness. Ephesians 6:4 says, "And you, fathers, do not provoke your children to wrath, but bring them up in the training and admonition of the Lord."

LIE #26: It's unnecessary to talk to my child about important issues because she shares my same beliefs.

Sometimes we fall into the trap of assuming our children share our beliefs on important issues. Satan makes us think they will automatically discern right from wrong simply because they have grown up in our homes.

You might think, *My child wouldn't dream of using drugs.* Or *I don't need to worry about my son having sex before marriage, because he knows it's a sin.* But remember, Satan's influence is strong. He will feed your child unbiblical ideas about his parents, other adults, drugs and alcohol, and life in general. At the same time the devil will seek to break your line of communication with your child and keep the two of you from discussing these life issues.

As I mentioned earlier in this chapter, when parents and children do not communicate regularly, they are left to guess about each other's feelings and ideas. So when you look to improve your communication with your child, don't forget its role in also influencing her beliefs.

LIE #27: Since I cannot sustain a long conversation with my child, there must be a problem.

Many forces hinder communication. Satan is the main threat, but our busy lives also contribute to the slow deterioration of communication lines.

One way to foster good communication with your child is to have a long-term outlook. Notice I didn't say a long conversation. In other words, don't measure the effectiveness of your communication by how long you can talk in one sitting. Instead, the frequency of positive exchanges should be your measuring stick. For the most part, any talking is better than none.

Rather than thinking, *Let's see if we can talk for five minutes*, view a dialogue as something you will accomplish over a period of time. In other words, continue a conversation over days, weeks, months. You can accomplish this by doing projects together that will require your being together over a period of time. Another way is to plan an upcoming event, such as a fishing trip or a trip to a ball game, or even to the mall. The anticipation of a continued conversation will help to form a better relationship.

This long-term outlook is also important when it comes to confrontations. There are times when confrontation and correction are necessary, but don't let those times slow the relationship you are building with your child. When you have had a confrontation, you be the one, when the time is right, to break the tension and return things back to normal. Your relationship with your child should be based on love and friendship—something to look forward to, not dread.

LIE #28: If I see things from my child's perspective, it will encourage more wild behavior.

The art of listening is one of the most overlooked ways of connecting with and helping our children. I cannot tell you how many kids have told me, "They just don't listen to me. Nothing I say means anything to them."

Listening to your child is important because you are the in-house physician, and with guidance from the Lord you are trying to help your child deal with the spiritual cancer that is destroying the family. You are there to gather information in order to make an accurate diagnosis and know what to pray for. And the more you listen, and the more they feel comfortable talking, the more information you will have to work with.

Seek to bond with your child and keep building your relationship, even if it is in small increments. I know it might be difficult even to have a desire for this bonding. The wild child inflicts a lot of pain on the family. She becomes a constant source of problems and conflict—an aggravation you feel like avoiding sometimes. The wild child is often deceitful, too, so that parents find themselves discounting or ignoring what she says. But this is another trap of the devil. Satan doesn't want parents and children to be on any level of communication because he knows this leads to healing.

Be your child's number one cheerleader in the game of life. You want her to do the right thing. You want her to make wise decisions. Watch for any glimpse of hope that she is maturing and growing into a responsible adult. Try to find areas of agreement. Many parents are afraid to do this. They think that if they agree with their wild child, the child will use this as more leverage and justification to do what they want. But the truth is, you can agree with and encourage a child's positive opinions and ideas without condoning bad behavior.

Coming to understand how your child thinks and reasons will provide a chance to teach her a better way. Remember, Satan is the Enemy and lies are his tools. He has deceived the wild child into believing that a particular behavior will satisfy a perceived need. Agreeing with your child can simply mean that you agree that she has a particular need. Once this is established, discuss her understanding of the need in a way that lets her know that you want to help. Talk about alternatives for meeting that need. Then you will be the one who administers advice, not Satan.

Despite all of the pain and disappointment the wild child brings into your life, seek to put yourself in her position. Think about the spiritual battle being waged in her soul. Think of the suffering and embarrassment she has experienced. Know that in times of confrontation the child's pain and frustration is usually speaking and not her better judgment. This is why non-confrontational conversation is especially important. Speak in a calm, friendly manner for a truer heart response from her.

You are not going to encourage bad behavior by becoming your child's friend. The closer she draws to you, the more you will become one in mind and spirit and the less she is going to want to disappoint you or let you down. As your child gets more in touch with her pain, as she becomes more communicative, you will both understand more clearly what to say to each other and be more comfortable saying it.

Many parents resist listening to the wild child because they feel that he is always manipulating them, trying to pull the wool over their eyes. Do you feel that your child is playing games? Do you have little or no patience for conversation because you don't believe everything he says? If so, you need to ask the Lord for a word of knowledge.

Proverbs 26:4 says, "Do not answer a fool according to his folly, lest you also be like him." On the other hand, Proverbs 26:5 says, "Answer a fool according to his folly, lest he be wise in his own eyes." You must pray for discernment to know which of these applies to your situation. Sometimes your child will be talking nonsense and foolishness and it is best to ignore it, while other times his foolishness needs to be addressed by godly counsel and even rebuke.

With Satan after your child's life, it is possible that he is simply misled in his opinions and ideas. The Bible says the mouth speaks from the overflow of the heart, and foolishness is bound up in the heart of a child (Matthew 12:34; Proverbs 22: 15). Take this into consideration when your child speaks. Understand that there is going to be some foolishness in his heart, even if it is only because he is young. Be ready to accept your parental responsibility to train your child and to teach him the wisdom that is from above.

Review Questions

1. Would you consider yourself as good a listener as a talker?
2. Do you fear that if you agree with your child's points of view, it will give her more freedom to rebel?
3. Are you holding a grudge against your child that prevents productive communication from taking place?
4. Are you doing what it takes to improve the quality of communication with your child?

Chemo-Prayers Time

Lie #24: Talking *to* the wild child is the same as communicating *with* the wild child.

Dear Lord, I thank you for the ability to communicate with my child. I pray that you would grant me the patience and love to exchange ideas and true feelings with my child. I pray that I would be able to acknowledge my shortcomings as well as issues that are preventing effective communication. Please give me a listening and compassionate ear to hear what my child is really saying. May Philippians 2:1–4 (NIV) be the passion of my heart when I talk with my child.

> If you have any encouragement from being united with Christ, if any comfort from his love, if any fellowship with the Spirit, if any tenderness and compassion, then make my joy complete by being like-minded, having the same love, being one in spirit and purpose. Do nothing out of selfish ambition or vain conceit, but in humility consider others better than yourselves. Each of you should look not only to your own interests, but also to the interests of others.

Lie #25: Even though my child and I don't talk much, we still have a strong relationship.

Dear God, please increase the amount of quality time I spend talking with my child. Please give me ideas on how to have more positive interactions. May I also have an increased desire to be closely involved in more areas of my child's life. Help me to recognize activities and interests that we can share together, so that our relationship continues to grow.

Lie #26: It's unnecessary to talk to my child about important issues because she shares my same beliefs.

Dear Lord, I pray that I would realize that nothing is automatic as it pertains to the beliefs of my child. I pray for the insight into how to discover what my child really believes about the important issues that will shape his/her life. More importantly, grant me the wisdom to teach my child the biblical principles that I believe are most important to his/her Christian development. Help me to be as diligent in my teaching as it says in Deuteronomy 6:6–9:

> And these words which I command you today shall be in your heart. You shall teach them diligently to your children, and shall talk of them when you sit in your house, when you walk by the way, when you lie down, and when you rise up. You shall bind them as a sign on your hand, and they shall be as frontlets between your eyes. You shall write them on the doorposts of your house and on your gates.

Lie #27: Since I cannot sustain a long conversation with my child, there must be a problem.

Dear Lord, please give me the wisdom to effectively use short conversations to communicate my heart with my child. I pray that I would build on these to develop a stronger relationship with my child. I pray that I would not focus on what could be wrong with our relationship but rather on how I can improve it by taking advantage of every communication opportunity, no matter how small.

Lie #28: If I see things from my child's perspective, it will encourage more wild behavior.

Dear Lord, thank you for your Word. I pray for the willingness to agree with my child even though I do not agree with many of the things he/she does. I pray that I could look past my frustration and anger and extend a compassionate ear to his/her views. Help me to realize that in some cases I could be wrong and I need to acknowledge this. I pray that I would realize there is more power in unity than in division and that I need to find common ground with my child. Amos 3:3 says, "Can two walk together, unless they are agreed?" The ultimate goal is to walk together. Help me find unity in the things we already agree on.

Chapter Seven

WILD THINKING: TURN STONES INTO BREAD?

CHANCES ARE YOU HAVE KNOWN someone who has had cancer. If the disease progresses, the person often loses his hair and much of his weight, and barely has the energy to walk around the house, if that. I have watched several people die of cancer, including a friend who played in the NFL.

At the time of his illness, Kurt was a defensive back for the Los Angeles Rams. He was absolutely the quickest and most athletic guy on the team. He was six feet tall, one hundred and eighty pounds, and quick as a cat. One day he went in for a typical examination for a minor injury, and cancer was diagnosed. When I visited him later, he was a mere shell of the world-class athlete I remembered.

My grandfather was my role model growing up, a man who loved his life. Even while in his seventies, he had the build of a thirty-five-year-old. But once cancer got hold of him, he wasted away to practically nothing. The last time I visited him it broke my heart. He passed away ten days later.

Through this book you have gotten to know Caroline. Before I went to her house to interview her, I wondered how the cancer had affected her body thus far. I didn't know what she would look like, so I prepared for the worst. She actually looked great. Other than her bald head, I didn't notice any signs of the disease or the treatment. But this was not the case from her point of view. She was suffering on the inside in a way I could not imagine.

During the interview I noticed that she kept wiping her eyes. I kept asking if she was okay, and she would say yes. Of all the questions I asked her, the one that drew the most emotion was "What is the hardest part of this whole ordeal?" She said she was tired of fighting and would have given up if it had not been for her four daughters. Death represented relief from her pain.

When you are with someone who has cancer, you must realize that you are seeing only the tip of the iceberg. Once cancer spreads, the body begins to deteriorate. Side effects of the medicine make matters worse, and the patient often reaches the point of wanting to give up.

In the same way, Satan can convince young people that they need to give up on being healed by God and take matters into their own hands.

When someone has been through a great deal of disappointment, pain, and grief, their desire for relief will begin to express itself. People will do almost anything to rid themselves of severe pain.

Your wild child makes many of the decisions he makes for this reason. Satan has convinced him that he needs to take matters into his own hands in order to deal with his uncomfortable, unfair, or unfortunate situation. In many cases legitimate pain exists, but in other situations, Satan has convinced your child that things are a lot worse than they really are. In either case, the devil is behind the scenes causing big-time problems. We get a glimpse into Satan's strategy in Matthew 4 when he talked with Jesus.

Jesus had been fasting for forty days and forty nights in the desert. The Bible tells us that He was hungry. Jesus' desire for food was a natural one. Satan seized the opportunity to tempt Jesus: "If You are the Son of God, command that these stones become bread" (Matthew 4:3). The devil basically told Jesus, *Use your power and influence to satisfy your needs from what is available. Since your need is a natural one and God is not meeting it, you don't need to wait any longer. God has given you the ability to take care of yourself. Use it. Turn the stones into bread!*

When a wild child rebels, he is in essence turning stones into bread. He is heeding the advice and encouragement of Satan to take matters into his own hands and satisfy a perceived need—all without God's guidance and direction.

So far in this book I have discussed twenty-eight lies that Satan aims at *parents*. In this chapter I will present six lies that Satan will tell the wild child in order to convince him or her to "turn stones into bread" and rebel against God. It is important for you, as a parent, to understand and pray against these tactics being used successfully against your child.

LIE #1: God is not going to take care of your needs.

When Satan challenged Jesus to take matters into His own hands and deny the lordship and control of God the Father, he was challenging the faithfulness of God to meet the needs of His Son. The devil insinuated that His Father had left Him alone to die of hunger and that God was not satisfying Jesus' natural desire for food. Therefore, Jesus needed to take care of it himself.

Satan uses the same lie today. He tells the wild child that God won't meet his emotional, physical, social, and spiritual needs. The devil tries to get our children (and us) to use whatever means possible to meet a natural desire or need. In essence, the devil tempts us to succumb to the lusts and desires of the flesh.

When you look at human behavior this way, it is easy to understand why people of all ages do the things they do. We actually believe we are simply doing the best we can to satisfy a legitimate need or desire. After all, Jesus was hungry. Why shouldn't He eat if He had the ability to get food? Young people have needs. Why shouldn't they satisfy those needs themselves?

In Matthew 6:30–33, Jesus tells us why we can and should rely on God:

> "Now if God so clothes the grass of the field, which today is, and tomorrow is thrown into the oven, will He not much more clothe you, O you of little faith? Therefore do not worry, saying, 'What shall we eat?' or 'What shall we drink?' or 'What shall we wear?' For after all these things the Gentiles seek. For your heavenly Father knows that you need all these things. But seek first the kingdom of God and His righteousness, and all these things shall be added to you."

LIE #2: Your life will always be filled with pain; therefore, embrace it.

Whenever the students walked into class, they seemed to avoid the right side of the room. They walked the few extra steps to avoid coming in contact with Evil Eye—a "gothic" student dressed in black, with white face paint, black makeup, and a stare that put everyone on edge.

You have likely seen gothic kids on school campuses, in malls, and elsewhere in your community. Gothics have been labeled as Satan worshipers and extra violent people, but this is not the whole story. In reality, their dress and behavior is the result of another lie of Satan.

Many of these kids have had painful experiences in life. They may have been abused, raped, had a friend who committed suicide, or lost a close family member to death. But as you and I know, these things happen to kids from all walks of life, and many of them turn out fine. They get involved in sports, extra-credit schoolwork, drama, or other school activities to make up for their pain. But gothics choose another way.

Satan has led these young people to believe that their mode of escape and protection is to *embrace the pain and to use it to their advantage*. In other words, if you can't beat it, join it. Satan has convinced them that pain is and always will be a part of their life. People will always let them down, and they need to isolate themselves from those who can hurt them. The black clothes, white faces, and deathlike makeup are used to intimidate people like you and me into staying away. The appearance of death and pain is their protective barrier.

Gothics are very introspective. While some kids bang their heads on the wall when listening to their music, gothics will stare at the wall as they contemplate their dismal plight. Satan has robbed them of any hope of the abundant life Jesus promises those who love Him. Satan has convinced them that death is their life.

What is so odd about these kids is that most come from homes with parents who are seemingly successful. In many cases, besides experiencing a traumatic event in their life, gothics have been neglected because of their parents' ambitions. In order to deal with the rejection and pain, these kids embrace this bizarre lifestyle. Satan has told them to turn stones into bread by displaying the dark side of life. Then Satan takes it a step further and makes the gothic culture seem welcoming to the many teenagers who are looking for some identity.

If your child has been pulled into this culture, it is important to look past his appearance and remember that behind the mask of death he is trying to display, there is a confused, lost kid who needs God. The problem is Satan has clouded your child's mind into thinking that the gothic lifestyle meets his needs. And once the devil accomplishes this, he will try to deceive your child into doing and accepting anything that goes along with this destructive lifestyle.

My friend Dave is a fellow pastor here in San Diego. Recently he told me about his experience ministering to a group of gothic kids at a local nightclub. It all started when he noticed a fifteen-year-old girl named Lythia drinking blood. Astonished by the sight, he asked Lythia and the others with her what they were doing. Their response shocked him. They said they were trying to turn into vampires and become *undead*.

Vampires are the ultimate example of a gothic. Supposedly because they have been dead once and cannot be killed again, they feel no pain. Drinking the blood of others perpetuates this state of being undead. If someone desires to be undead, not only does he fully embrace the theory of being a victim of constant pain and rejection, but he also cannot be hurt again. Vampires have fully conquered the victim status and used it to their advantage. To take this one step further, drinking blood is a counterfeit Communion in the sense that the blood of others gives them freedom from death. Satan tells these young people that once they have drunk the blood and attained the vampire status, they can acquire new power to control those who have been in control of their lives.

Dave was determined to minister to Lythia. He knew that behind the black clothes and stark makeup was a little girl who needed to know the love of Jesus. Not wanting to come off as the preacher that he was, Dave started by simply asking Lythia questions, such as, why was she drinking blood? And, wasn't she concerned about getting AIDS?

Lythia was very defensive. Before Dave had even said much, she accused him of automatically viewing her as a Satan worshiper. But Dave, knowing better, accused her of judging him without knowing who he was or what was in his heart. He told her she was being just as hypocritical as the people she was trying to avoid. When Lythia realized that Dave was right, she warmed up to him.

Over the next several weeks Dave returned to the nightclub regularly to talk with Lythia and her friends. The relationship developed, and then one night he had the opportunity to talk with them about the apocalypse. Because gothics are very much into the annihilation of the world, the Bible's teaching on the end times is a very interesting topic. As Lythia and her friends learned what the Bible says about the end of the world, they were confronted with the question: How were they going to prepare for the return of Christ? Lythia consequently received the Lord, left the gothic scene, and is now attending college and studying dance and writing poetry.

LIE #3: The benefits of meeting your own needs outweigh the consequences.

Young people have many God-given desires that Satan targets and attempts to exploit. He tells children that God has forgotten about them, their parents have forgotten about them, and that they need to satisfy their own desires—now! The devil backs this up with the same lie he told Adam and Eve: "You will not surely die." In other words, "Don't worry. There won't be any consequences. Look, everyone is doing it. Everyone is happy and enjoying himself. God is holding out on you." In light of this so-called logic, it's not surprising that Satan snares so many young people, especially those who do not have prayer support, godly examples in the home, and godly friends who will encourage them to do the right thing.

LIE #4: Why use your strengths for godly purposes when they can be used to meet your own needs?

You have heard it said that Satan tempts us in our weaknesses and that he tries to take advantage of our sense of yearning or needing something. But this is only part of the truth. He also tempts us to use our strengths for ungodly purposes. For instance, he will tell people with a sense of humor to use their gift to get what they want or need. Or he will tell pretty girls to use their beauty and charm to get what they want or think they need.

Natalia was a typical teenage girl who had everything going for her. Her family thought she was doing great, but little did they know about the time bomb ticking in her heart and mind. She started slipping in high school, getting poor grades for four straight years. Somehow she made it into college, but kept dropping out. In a short span of time she broke up with her boyfriend and stopped going to church, and her mom suffered from depression and was not able to be a support to her.

Natalia turned to alcohol and cocaine. At night she drank until she couldn't drink any more, then did cocaine in order to get a second wind to start drinking again. During this same time she was having sex with guys she had no serious feelings for. One night while drunk she told a guy how much she wanted to go out with him, bragging how she could please him and make him feel good. His response shocked her: "Why should I like you? You don't even like yourself."

Natalia stepped back and looked at her life. *Why am I always getting drunk, or high, or having sex? Why am I so afraid of being alone and needing always to be around lots of people?* Natalia realized the guy was right: she didn't like herself. She felt empty. Even though she had gone to church with her parents, she didn't have a faith she could call her own. Add to that the loss of her boyfriend and her mom's support. She had so much pain that drinking and getting high were the only remedies she knew. She did not know where or how to belong, but she wanted to. Her soul needs were crying out for attention, and Satan provided options to meet those needs. But after turning countless stones into bread, she was left with the same emptiness she had started with.

The good news is that Natalia was drawn back to church and the Bible to find the very answers the converted stones could not provide. And once she found the Lord and surrendered her life to Him, her addictions ended and the empty spot in her life was filled.

Humpty Dumpty sat on a wall,
Humpty Dumpty had a great fall,
All the king's horses and all the king's men,
Couldn't put Humpty together again.

The problem is Humpty Dumpty didn't need the king's horses or the king's men; he needed the real King, Jesus. The same is true for the wild child. When he suffers a great fall,

Satan will offer him everything short of the King.

Satan will give children a false sense of their abilities and cause them to believe they can do things they cannot or should not do. This is why you will see a wild child driving full speed down a dead-end street in total denial that there is a barricade at the end of the road. He has been falsely convinced that he can make it through without being harmed. This is also why you will see kids do weird things like taking drugs the night before an exam, having sex immediately after finding out their partner has a sexually transmitted disease, or hanging out with friends who they know are in trouble with the police. Satan will convince young girls that beauty and sex appeal alone are enough to land a guy who will take care of them and satisfy all of their needs. The devil will convince students that they only need to study one hour for an exam when, in fact, they need three days.

LIE #5: There's no need to resist temptations.

Once Satan identifies a lust or perceived need of the flesh in a teenager, he can bring irresistible temptations into that child's life in order to convince him to turn stones into bread.

In the book of James, we get a clear sense of what temptation truly is:

> Let no one say when he is tempted, "I am tempted by God"; for God cannot be tempted by evil, nor does He Himself tempt anyone. But each one is tempted when he is drawn away by his own desires and enticed. Then, when desire has conceived, it gives birth to sin; and sin, when it is full-grown, brings forth death. (James 1:13–15)

From this passage we learn that God tempts no one. Thus, if

your child falls into temptation, do not blame God for the pain in your child's life. As James says, God is not tempted by evil, and He does not use evil as one of his tools. Instead, all of us are drawn away by our own desires. In other words, our sinful nature, which is at war with the spirit of God, is enticed into doing something sinful and rebellious.

Satan makes false promises. He leads the wild child into believing that the grass on the other side of the fence is not only greener but that it is also healthier and softer. Satan tells young people that drugs will set them free from their problems, that their perceived need for a family will be met by joining a gang. He tells them that breaking the law together with someone else will replace the bond they should be getting from their family. He will tell teenagers that they can be happy just by getting high and that their ability to party, bum money from people, and live from place to place will satisfy them enough.

Satan will even create an urgent need when none exists and then make false promises for meeting that need. That explains why some young people who have a great childhood feel the need to take drugs; why some kids who have two parents at home and a good family life get into gangs; and why girls who have everything to live for still sleep around in order to feel loved.

Young people are especially vulnerable to sexual desires and temptations. In the Song of Solomon, we are told, "I charge you, O daughters of Jerusalem, by the gazelles or by the does of the field, do not stir up nor awaken love until it pleases" (3: 5). In other words, don't disturb the "love juices" until there is a biblical relationship to pour them into. Satan will begin to identify and magnify these desires whenever he can get the opportunity, whether it is through pornography, molestation, or premarital sexual activity. Once a teenager is exposed to these feelings, the feelings take on a mind and life of their own. They begin to dictate to your child his perceived needs and wants.

One of the most destructive addictions has nothing to do with drugs or alcohol. It is pornography. This became evident to me while counseling an adult friend whose addiction to pornography was destroying his marriage and family.

As he poured out his heart to me, he talked about the frustration and pain he felt by being trapped. He perceived that he was totally helpless and hopeless of ever being set free.

"Miles," he said, "I wouldn't wish this on any kid."

I think of that friend's comment every time I speak with young people who find themselves in the pornography trap.

This was the case with Carlos. When he was fifteen he stumbled across some pornographic magazines. Needless to say, the pictures were just what his young sex drive craved. It is obvious from the billion-dollar porn industry that boys and men are very susceptible to this kind of information and publication, and Carlos was no different. One look became another look and then another until he found himself addicted.

As you read this book, you may be wondering if your son is doing this. Where might he be getting the pornography? That was one of my first questions to Carlos. He found the magazines in his stepdad's closet. His father was supplying him with the very weapon that was destroying his life, and he didn't even know it.

The trap and consequences of pornography don't stop with an addiction to looking at the pictures. It spills over into the mind and heart. Carlos began masturbating while looking at the magazines, fantasizing about the women in the pictures. This became a regular occurrence and added excitement to it while deepening his addiction. This went on for more than three years. Carlos began lusting after the girls in his school, putting their faces on the images in the magazines.

Matthew 5:28 says that if a man lusts in his heart after a woman, he has sinned. But that's not what Satan was telling Carlos. The devil was saying things like "It's okay, Carlos. You won't get caught and there are no consequences. After all, you're a man and this is what men do. That's why your stepdad has the magazines." The devil gets the wild child to play an evil game of truth or dare: *Do I believe what my parents are telling me, that the Bible is truth? Or do I dare follow the crowd and the exciting road of life? Do I believe the self-proclaimed truth of the Bible along with its rules and regulations, or do I dare to make my own decisions, based on my own interpretation of life? After all, I do have needs, feelings, desires, and wants. And they must be from God because he made me.*

The wild child doesn't know who to believe: authority figures, God and the Christian point of view, or the devil who brings with him the appearance of fun and excitement. Mix in the naturally adventurous spirit of a teenager and his need to discover all that life offers, and you have a volatile combination.

Although Carlos's mother was unaware of her son's addictions, she prayed for him and tried to get him to go to church with her. Meanwhile, Carlos was beginning to realize that he couldn't say no to the lure of the porno magazines, masturbation, and the thoughts that accompanied them. He tried to see how long he could avoid the magazines, but it never lasted more than several days. What worried Carlos even more was the fact that he had a little brother in the house who might fall into the same trap.

Carlos finally gave in to his mother's wishes and started to go to church every once in a while. He enjoyed it, but stopped going for some reason and continued to feed his destructive addictions. One day Carlos was working out when he suffered a stroke. After tests were run, it was discovered that he had a birth defect that predisposed him to having a stroke. Carlos was temporarily paralyzed on one side and in the hospital for over three weeks.

The incident scared Carlos, and he decided to try church again and ask God to give him another chance. He wanted to escape the trap of pornography and knew he needed to change. When he picked up a Bible, it fell open to the story of the woman who was instantly healed of a hemorrhage. He saw in it the irony that a stroke is caused by a hemorrhage in the brain. Soon afterward he trusted his life to the hands of Jesus and has since broken free of pornography and masturbation.

Carlos realizes that he paid a big price for his sin and knows that he was in the spiritual battle of his life, but he still feels Satan trying to lure him back into the old lifestyle. Carlos knows it is a worthless pursuit, but the temptation is constant and strong. I encouraged him to find someone to hold him accountable. Understandably, he said he was embarrassed to talk about it with anyone. I explained to him that 1 Corinthians 10: 13 says, "No temptation has overtaken you except such as is common to man; but God is faithful, who will not allow you to be tempted beyond what you are able, but with the temptation will also make the way of escape, that you may be able to bear it."

Not only do parents need to be sensitive to the flesh and soul desires of their children but also to the fact that Satan can use things around the house to get children to meet those desires: guns, alcohol, drugs, television, music, and even magazines.

LIE #6: If you don't take control of your life, you are a chump.

Satan will challenge your child's identity. Need proof? Just reread what he said to the King of Kings as he tried to tempt Jesus to turn stones into bread: "If You are the Son of God . . ." The key word in this phrase is *if*. Satan challenged Jesus' identity—in other words, His pride. He told Jesus to prove His power. The devil will say to the wild child: *Who are you, really? If you are so powerful and independent and sure of yourself, prove it.* The less secure your child is about who he is in the Lord and who he is in his relationship with you and the rest of the family, the more likely will he be to fall for this trap. Satan also tells kids that rebelling against their parents will help them develop an identity of their own.

For most of Peter's young life, rebellion and making a name for himself were the norm. For his first nine years his family lived in Lebanon, where conflicts with Israeli police were common. Though he was quite young, Peter participated in demonstrations, throwing rocks at the Israeli police and running through fresh tear gas. When the family moved to East Los Angeles, conditions were not all that different. In L.A., rather than Israelis against Syrians, it was Americans against other Americans: Hispanic, Asian, White, and Black. As the new kid on the block from another culture and a land far away, Peter did not immediately fit in, but he was determined to make his mark. Rebellion and violence would be his tools.

Whenever Peter did something, he did it in a way that would never be forgotten. He was an extremist, to say the least. When he was thirteen, someone challenged him to ignite a stick of dynamite in a crowd. It left twelve people with temporary hearing problems. Later he was involved in drive-by shootings. At school he got in fights regularly. He'd get caught drinking in school or showing up already drunk. In one two-month period he was suspended each week. It reached the point where Peter's parents felt they had no other choice but to send him to a boarding school in Cyprus, Greece. They thought two months of discipline away from his surroundings would change his attitude, but it didn't work. Peter returned to Los Angeles and began abusing heroin. His habit became so bad that he even attempted to kill himself.

You might be asking yourself why someone would live such a life. The closest answer Peter can give is that he was angry with his father. He did not have a good relationship with him, and his dad had never told him he loved him. According to Peter, his rebellious actions were in response to the rejection he perceived from the number one person he needed and wanted to love him. In a very distorted way, Peter was trying to get the attention of his dad, but why choose such a destructive manner? I can answer that in one word: Satan.

It's difficult to know whether or not Peter's dad truly rejected him. In the end, what matters is that Satan used Peter's sense of rejection as a tool to deceive and entice him into doing the things he did. I know without a doubt that when Peter surrendered his life to Christ, the rebellious behavior stopped.

It happened while Peter was at a Christian recovery center trying to break his heroin addiction. The second evening there, sitting on a prayer rock, Peter accepted Christ as his Savior. Normally it takes at least two weeks for the intense withdrawal symptoms to disappear, but Peter slept soundly through that night. His turnaround was so miraculous that even medical professionals cannot explain it. Peter is now completely sober and establishing a strong relationship with his father.

For Peter, the ultimate acquisition of identity and power

came in his ultimate act of weakness: surrendering his life to Jesus. It may seem like your son is fighting something—mad at the world—when, in fact, he is turning stones into bread to satisfy his desire for power.

None of this is new or unique to your child. These tricks of Satan are as old as time itself. But the good news is that our Father will fulfill and satisfy our needs and our children's needs. After Satan tempted Jesus to turn stones into bread, Jesus replied, "It is written, 'Man shall not live by bread alone, but by every word that proceeds from the mouth of God' " (Matthew 4:4). What Jesus said is the ultimate goal for parents of a wild child: Satisfaction in life comes from obeying God.

Pray that your child develops such a relationship with God that when he is faced with a decision or need he will look to his heavenly Father for the solution. Pray that your child will be able to distinguish between Satan's deception and God's faithful promises, and that instead of turning to drugs, sex, gangs, and violence, he will turn to the Lord.

Review Questions

1. What does your child think he needs in life?
2. In what ways is he trying to meet those needs?
3. What are the false promises being made to your child?

Chemo-Prayers Time

Lie #1: God is not going to take care of your needs.

Dear Lord, thank you for your Word. I pray that my child will realize that you promise to take care of all of our needs. Matthew 6:30 says, "Now if God so clothes the grass of the field, which today is, and tomorrow is thrown into the oven, will He not much more clothe you, O you of little faith?" Lord, I pray that you would supernaturally reveal this to my child. I pray that the lie Satan is using to trick my child into taking matters into his/her own hands would be disarmed by the truth of your Word. I pray that my example of dependence on you will display this faithfulness to my family.

Lie #2: Your life will always be filled with pain; therefore, embrace it.

Dear Lord, I thank you that you promise to deliver us from pain and misery. You have promised an abundant life to those who trust YOU; therefore, I will trust you and expect to experience the abundant life that you promise. You also tell us in Isaiah 25:8 that you wipe away every tear from our eyes. I will hold onto this promise and wait for its fulfillment in my life.

Lie #3: The benefits of meeting your own needs outweigh the consequences.

Dear Lord, thank you for your Word. I know that Romans 6:23 says very clearly that the penalty of sin is death. Today I would like to ask you to reveal this truth to my child. Please help him/her to see the deception of Satan. Please show my child that he has been lying to him/her all this time and that the life my child is living is merely an existence, not the abundant life you promise. I pray that I can continue to pray this until I see a repentant heart in my child.

Lie #4: Why use your strengths for godly purposes when they can be used to meet your own needs?

Dear Lord, thank you for your Word. I pray that my child would realize that he/she has been blinded by the Evil One. My child has no idea how deceived he/she is and how helpless he/she is to meet needs in his/her own power. I pray that my child's eyes would be opened that he/she may truly and sincerely realize the need for you in his/her life.

Ephesians 4:17–19, says "No longer walk as the rest of the

Gentiles walk, in the futility of their mind, having their under-standing darkened, being alienated from the life of God, be-cause of the ignorance that is in them, because of the blindness of their heart; who, being past feeling, have given themselves over to lewdness, to work all uncleanness with greediness."

Lord, please open my child's heart so that he/she will see his own weaknesses and need for you. And give me the wisdom to minister to my child when he/she begins to see the truth.

Lie #5: There's no need to resist temptations.

Dear Lord, thank you for your Word. I pray against the false promises Satan is using to entice my child. Lord, the Bible clearly says that Satan is a liar and that the truth is not in him. In John 8:44–45, Jesus tells those who oppose Him, "You are of your father the devil, and the desires of your father you want to do. He was a murderer from the beginning, and does not stand in the truth, because there is no truth in him. When he speaks a lie, he speaks from his own resources, for he is a liar and the father of it." Lord, please reveal to my child that Satan will never keep one of those false promises he is making to him/her. And when my child realizes this, may I be ready to love and accept him/her.

Lie #6: If you don't take control of your life, you are a chump.

Dear Lord, thank you for your Word. Lord, I pray that my child would humble himself/herself and surrender his/her life to you. I know that only in humility are we honored with life. Mark 8:35–37 says, "For whoever desires to save his life will lose it, but whoever loses his life for My sake and the gospel's will save it. For what will it profit a man if he gains the whole world, and loses his own soul? Or what will a man give in exchange for his soul?" Lord, give my child the humility to let go and to let you be God.

WILD DADS:
MEN OF GOD

AS I MENTIONED EARLIER, when Caroline woke up after her first surgery, she was expecting to be able to go home and get on with her life. Instead, she was told the cancer was worse than anticipated. It was in her lymph system, which usually means trouble.

Caroline immediately sought out the best doctor she could find. She wanted one from the hospital that had been caring for her, because the staff had treated her so well. In addition, she changed her insurance coverage to ensure the opportunity to pick any doctor from within the system that she felt could best serve her needs. She wanted one who would be strong and decisive.

When people get sick, especially if hospitalization is necessary, they become very dependent on their doctors. Friends don't always know how to react to serious illnesses. Some back away, afraid of saying or doing the wrong thing. Others offer well-meaning but often useless or redundant advice. But a patient's doctor becomes her primary source of strength, experience, and knowledge. He does the research, anticipates problems, and prepares to take decisive action on behalf of his patient. For these reasons, a good doctor will be looked to for direction and encouragement. He will be objective about treatment because his number one goal is to heal.

In Caroline's case, the doctor had to tell her the cancer had spread to her spinal fluid, and then that she had about six months to live. With a husband and four daughters, this, of course, was devastating news. Caroline's doctor did everything he could do. He opened her skull and placed a shunt in her head in the hope that the treatment would bring results. When this didn't help, he administered medicine directly into her spine to treat the cancer. The doctor is the one who bears a patient's burden of discouragement and disappointment in the face of bad news. Needless to say, he has to be a rock.

Caroline could change her insurance in order to find the best doctor, but your child doesn't have that option. She cannot pick the most experienced and knowledgeable parents available. She is stuck with you! Therefore, you need to work to be the best parents possible. You need to be a rock for her.

In this chapter, I want to challenge you dads in your role in the family. Even though I know there are moms out there who are doing a tremendous job in the home, and some of you all alone, I want to encourage dads to be godly—for one simple reason: When a dad is righteous and fulfills his role in the home, he is God's most powerful agent for change.

If you are a single mom, you might be thinking, *There's no dad in the life of my child.* Or when he is around, *He's far from being a godly example.* I challenge you to believe that God will not ignore the individual needs of your child, and the more clearly and powerfully you can by faith pray for those needs, the more quickly they can be addressed. God can do even more than change the heart of a dad. He can bring other mentors or role models into the life of your child—a teacher, a coach, an employer, a neighbor, or a pastor.

In Genesis 21, Hagar experienced a similar situation. Being the mother of Abraham's first son, Ishmael, you might think she would have been taken care of, but this was not the case. Once Abraham had his son of faith, Isaac, the problems began. As a result, Hagar was sent away with her son to live the life of a single mother. Ishmael and Isaac began to experience normal sibling rivalries, and the two mothers had issues between them. When Hagar was tired, discouraged, and ready to give up, she and her son cried unto the heavens and God heard them. God not only promised to take care of her son but also to bless him abundantly.

When there is a shortage of men in the life of your child, the church should come forward to provide male mentors and elders for them.

LIE #29: The dad should depend on someone else, including the mom, to be the lead investigator in finding a cure for the wild child's cancer.

More than anyone on this planet, a dad can be used by God to change a child. This does not mean that he will be the only one to bring about change, but he will be the one who has the most influence in the entire process of a child's transformation. He is the one who will recruit and challenge others to help his child in areas beyond his expertise. He will be the major support of these people with wisdom and insight about his child.

When a child decides to repent and come back home, it needs to be the dad whom she finds looking for her, waiting to receive her, forgive her, and throw a party.

In Luke 15, there is a familiar story of a wild child who wanted his own way. The Bible refers to him as the prodigal son. The passage is also known as the story of the forgiving father.

Instead of waiting for the proper time to receive his inheritance from his father, the young man decided to ask for it early and to go away and live his life on his own. This broke his father's heart, but he honored his son's wishes and gave him the money. After a period of time, the son, not knowing how to manage money, or life in general, found himself in a bad situation. He had spent everything and was without friends or employment. So he decided to go home and be a servant in his father's household.

The story vividly describes the love of a dad looking for his lost son, one who was ready to forgive and forget. But it also gives us insight into the characteristics of a dad who dealt successfully with a wild child.

The first thing I will mention is that the prodigal's father was committed to providing for his family. The Bible calls him the "priest" of the home—from the Latin word for *bridge builder*. The father builds and represents the bridge between God and the family. It is his example of love, concern, authority, and leadership that reveals to the family the heart of God.

The most obvious evidence of this is the fact that God gave dads His own title: Father. The name carries with it great responsibility, and each father needs to acknowledge and accept this responsibility. This is not to imply that if your child is failing in life it is your fault, but it is definitely designed to send this message: As the father, you are God's representative in the home. You are the symbol of God's power, love, authority, and compassion. You have the responsibility to represent His love, patience, forgiveness, and faithfulness. But of all these qualities, there is one that stands out more than the rest. It is the quality of being steadfast and firm—a *rock*.

Throughout the Bible, God is referred to as the "rock." This term implies something immovable, secure, dependable, a sure foundation on which to step out. As a rock, Dad, your commitment to God must be unchangeable and your resistance to wild child behavior must be consistent and solid.

The Bible describes Jesus as the rock in several ways. In Psalm 18:2, He is referred to as our deliverer: "The Lord is my rock and my fortress and my deliverer; my God, my strength, in whom I will trust; my shield and the horn of my salvation, my stronghold."

In Psalm 31:2, we're told that in times of trouble, Jesus is the rock of our defense. It says, "Bow down Your ear to me, deliver me speedily; be my rock of refuge, a fortress of defense to save me." In Psalm 95:1, Jesus is our Savior: "Oh come, let us sing to the Lord! Let us shout joyfully to the Rock of our salvation." In 1 Corinthians 10:4, Jesus is the rock from which life comes: "For they drank of that spiritual Rock that followed them, and that Rock was Christ."

But the Bible also says that Jesus is the rock with whom the buck stops. Matthew 21:44 says, "And whoever falls on this stone will be broken; but on whomever it falls, it will grind him to powder."

These are attributes that should also be ascribed to an earthly father. He is someone who will protect, deliver, and save.

There are two nonnegotiable, unchangeable, immovable facts that should be associated with every father. First is a dad's commitment to love God. This simply requires a father to be totally dependent upon the Father for strength, wisdom, patience, and everything necessary to produce a man of God. Matthew 22:37–38 says, "You shall love the Lord your God with all your heart, with all your soul, and with all your mind. This is the first and great commandment." A dad must be constantly and consistently growing in the grace and knowledge of his Lord and Savior Jesus Christ. There is simply no way that a man can fulfill the responsibilities of being a father, much less help a wild child to get back on the right road of life, unless he is walking in the light provided by fellowship with the heavenly Father.

The second responsibility of a dad is very simple. It is a commitment to love your neighbor—or family members, in this case. Matthew 22:39–40 says, "And the second is like it: 'You shall love your neighbor as yourself.' On these two commandments hang all the Law and the Prophets."

LIE #30: The dad is not responsible for his child's behavior.

It is true that our kids are free-will agents and must be responsible for their own actions. It is also true that there is only so much you can do to stop a child from being wild. But on the other hand, you as a dad have a mandate from God to train up a child in the way that she should go. It is also true that our number one commandment is to love our child as we would love ourselves. This means that we should work just as hard at helping and training our children to obey God as we do ourselves.

Ron never dreamed he would someday learn how to administer a drug test, but it became necessary when his oldest son began using drugs. As a result, Ron became very sensitive to the damage drugs can inflict on a family. Therefore, he decided to implement a new rule in his home. On any given day he might administer a drug test. His sons know they are never out of range for being tested for drugs and alcohol. They have no choice but to submit. Even though few, if any, of their friends face the possibility of a home drug test, they trust their dad. These young men know that their dad loves God and is committed to being a godly man. They are confident that their dad is doing what he believes God is leading him to do. They also know that after watching what happened to their brother, their dad is doing what he thinks is necessary to prevent any more pain in the family.

When your child looks to you, she needs to believe two things. First: *My dad is committed to God. Whether right or wrong, whether I agree or disagree, he is committed to God and His will for our family.* The second thing your child must know is: *My dad is committed to helping us to obey God. He really loves us and is doing what he absolutely believes God wants him to do.*

It is vital for all fathers to fully understand and accept this role for their lives. But why is the dad's involvement so crucial?

LIE #31: Moms and dads have the same influence on children.

After a recent high school football game, I observed something very interesting. A particular running back had just had a great game, and both of his parents came on the field to congratulate him. When the mom approached her son, she gave him a big hug and kiss and told him what a great job he had done. He thanked her, but then she kept complimenting him over and over again. When our moms say "good job," what do we find ourselves saying? "C'mon, Mom. You always say that." And that is exactly what the football player said. But when his dad came over, he looked intently for approval. I could tell he wanted more than anything to hear his dad say, "Good job, son." Why is this? Why do we want so badly to please our dads?

For nine months we were in our mother's womb. We were not only physically but emotionally attached to her. When we were born, it was our mom who fed us, cared for us, and gave us the daily nurturing love we needed. An indescribable bond was established from day one. This bond continued to be strengthened throughout our young childhood. But then we come to realize that there is another person in the house, someone who represents the other half of our makeup: Dad. Who is this guy, and does he love me?

As we grow, we begin to develop a relationship with this man, and we begin to learn about who we are through this relationship. Throughout our growth and development, it is this man's approval that becomes so vital to our sense of worth and identity. It is this man who will validate us as we mature. It is the dad who helps his daughters to become young ladies and his sons to become young men.

My first two children are girls, and when they were young I started a yearly tradition of buying them dresses for Christmas. Shopping for the dresses was not the fun part (I hate shopping), but I loved it when they would come out of their rooms and twirl around, showing off for the man they wanted to please. I was the man who was showing them how to be a lady. I was the man who was validating them along with their mother.

I have a different role with my son. I must train and model for him what a man is supposed to be. As a boy, he must learn from a man what it means to be a man. He must learn to be responsible, caring, and reliable. It takes a man to affirm this growth in his life. It requires a man to model this to him as he develops. And it takes a man to assist him in growing out of boyhood (when he does what he *wants* to do) and into a man (when he does what he *must* do).

Only a father can accomplish these things for his family.

Many fathers are not living at home, and this is nothing short of a tragedy for his children. Yes, many kids have made it without their dads, but there is absolutely no substitute for the loving, caring, involved, at-home dad. If you are a dad, please take to heart what I will say in these next few pages, because Satan would want nothing more than for you to be ignorant of these things.

A very close friend of mine is addicted to alcohol and cocaine. He has three children under the age of seven. He has been in denial about the effects of his habits for many years. He thinks his lifestyle is normal and acceptable, simply because he has been able to sustain a good living. But I have watched and listened to his family die a slow death. His wife, needing his income simply to feed her children, is operating on her last nerve. He stays out for days at a time and comes home hung over, thinking everything will go on as usual. He spends about a thousand dollars a week on his habit, leaving very little extra income for his family. Not only is there little money left over but there is also less of him. In name and title he is the father of his children, but in function he is barely a live-in big brother.

I am most concerned about his daughter, who is the oldest and most aware about what is going on. She has become more and more angry and stressed. She lashes out at her mom and brothers. She is beginning to refer to her father as always being drunk, never being home, and never having time for them. The really sad part about this situation is that my friend does not see the connection between his problems and his daughter's behavior. Little does he realize that he is the example of God to his children.

> Or what man is there among you who, if his son asks for bread, will give him a stone? Or if he asks for a fish, will he give him a serpent? If you then, being evil, know how to give good gifts to your children, how much more will your Father who is in heaven give good things to those who ask Him! (Matthew 7:9–11)

In this passage, Jesus teaches us to depend on the Father in heaven for all good things. The things we get from our earthly fathers are mere shadows of the things we should expect from our heavenly Father.

The Bible mandates that fathers provide certain things for their families. First Timothy 5:8 says, "But if anyone does not provide for his own, and especially for those of his household, he has denied the faith and is worse than an unbeliever." Of course a dad needs to provide the basics, such as clothes, food, and shelter. But children need so much more. They need the dad's presence in the home to represent the love and security of the Lord. They need the dad to be there to provide an environment in which they can be nurtured and develop into responsible adults. If a man cannot provide a safe and loving environment for his wife and children, he is no better than an unbeliever.

A good father needs to be a man of honor. When the wild child in Luke 15 realized that he had messed up, the first thing he thought about was his dad, and that if he confessed to his dad—a godly man, a man of honor—he could expect forgiveness and acceptance back into the family.

In his book *21 Laws of Leadership*, John Maxwell, bestselling author and expert on leadership training, spells out five reasons why people will follow you or obey your commands. At first, Maxwell's insights appear to only reflect the business world. However, as I will explain, I believe they can teach us about our roles as fathers.

The five reasons why people will follow you are:

1. Your position and the authority that comes with that position;
2. Your relationship with that person;
3. What you have done for the company or organization to which you both belong;
4. What you have done for that person as an individual; and
5. Who you are as a person.

This last point is the most significant and long-term reason why someone will look up to you. They respect your integrity and personhood so much that they are willing to follow you through a wall. This comes from nothing but respect of character.

It is so very important for dads to have secure relationships with God the Father. It will only be through this strong relationship that you will be able to properly represent and fulfill the title of father. Every day of your life your actions are teaching a lesson to your kids about life's priorities. They are developing values for their own lives by watching how you interact with people, with them (your children), and the world around you.

You should not strive to force your child to listen to you because you are the dad, or because you pay the bills, or because you brought her into this world. Your child should listen to you, follow you, and obey you because of who you are as a person. The only way as a parent to establish this kind of respect is to live above reproach. There is a big problem if you think you can fake this, because you cannot. Your child knows your good and bad traits. Your friends don't know what you are like behind closed doors, and they don't really know how your prayer life is or how you act when you are irritated. They don't really know how humble and generous you are, but your child knows all of these things. She knows what your real priorities are. She knows where she stands in relation to your job, your friends, and your hobbies.

Whenever I can minister to the child of a pastor, I jump at the chance for two very strong reasons. First, if I can lighten the load of a fellow minister, it can transfer into hundreds and sometimes thousands of other people getting better care. But my second reason is somewhat selfish. As a minister myself, I hope someone will take special interest in my children in their times of need. Families of ministers come under extraordinary spiritual attack, and the children often suffer the fallout.

A while ago I was talking with the child of a local pastor. This pastor was well known in his community and had a great reputation, but his children were not walking with the Lord. When I began talking to this particular child about his life and struggles, I asked him why he was not walking with the Lord. His response shocked me: "I couldn't believe that stuff, because I know my dad, and he is a hypocrite. He preaches righteousness to the people who don't see him at home. He doesn't really live that way when no one is around. He is rude to all of us at home. He doesn't have time for us and our problems, only for the people at the church."

Dad, your actions speak so loud that nothing you say can out-shout the message of what you do. In other words, your promises, family lectures, and sermons mean nothing compared to your love toward your child in the form of action.

LIE #32: A dad does not have to be a man of honor in order to be honored by his kids.

It is the dad who is a man of honor whose kids will honor him. This was exactly what happened when Abraham was commanded by God to kill his one and only son, Isaac. As they walked up the mountain, Isaac saw the wood and he saw the fire, but he did not see anything for the sacrifice. When he asked his dad about it, Abraham told him that God himself would provide the sacrifice. Isaac trusted and respected his dad so much that he lay on the wood and watched his dad raise his hand to kill him, and as far as we know, he did not put up a fight (Genesis 22:1–14).

A father of honor needs to develop an environment where conflict resolution is nurtured. This does not mean a place where there is no conflict at all, but a place where conflict is dealt with in a biblical manner. First Timothy 3:2–5 says,

> A bishop then must be blameless, the husband of one wife, temperate, sober-minded, of good behavior, hospitable, able to teach; not given to wine, not violent, not greedy for money, but gentle, not quarrelsome, not covetous; one who rules his own house well, having his children in submission with all reverence.

The last line in this passage mentions the word *rule*, which implies to manage and resolve conflicts and differences. As a father, you must be able to act as the voice of reason and confront the issues that are dividing the family. Of course, this is easier said than done. That's why for the rest of this chapter I will discuss the key steps to helping the wild child, starting with being involved in your child's life.

LIE #33: You can be a good dad without being an involved dad.

Satan will try to lure you away from being involved in your child's life because that reduces your opportunity to confront family issues.

Jake was one of those dads who went to work, came home, ate dinner, read the paper, and then went to bed. He got the *Reader's Digest* version of the home happenings from his wife and then ruled with an iron fist. This is what he thought was the manly thing to do. But Jake did not truly understand the issues. He didn't really know the facts. This sent the sad but true message to Jake's family that he didn't really care. His family was like one of the departments in Jake's company. *Give me the bottom line so I can rule, because I really don't have the time to get involved.* Let me tell you something: Real dads are involved.

Proverbs 18:13 says that it is foolish and even shameful to answer a matter before you hear it. Don't overreact when things are said or done. The home of the God-fearing dad must be a place where a child is free to express her opinions and to talk about what's going on in her life without fear of being shot down or suffering consequences.

As I mentioned earlier, my daughter had been bugging me to get her a pet for some time, so on her birthday we finally bought a bird for her. She was told that to stop a bird from biting people who hold it, the bird should be dropped to the floor whenever it bit someone. Well, my daughter started to use this strategy, until one day after dropping the bird, she noticed it had drawn up one of its legs toward its body. The bird hopped around on one leg, not letting the left one touch the ground. Something was obviously wrong, but we couldn't figure out what. Normally the bird would squawk whenever anyone was around, but now she didn't let out a peep. If she were really hurt, we thought she'd be constantly squawking.

When we finally took the bird to the vet, he said that her leg was broken, and then he explained why she hadn't squawked. When animals are hurt, he said, they don't attract attention to themselves because of the danger associated with it. Having a predator aware of your weakness is the last thing you want, because it could spell the end of your life.

As humans, especially family members, we need to depend on and take advantage of our ability to help one another. But the reality of the situation is that many kids will hold their pain inside because they know how we parents will react.

LIE #34: A strong dad does not have to listen to the opinion of his kids. His opinion is the law.

Jimmy was having a problem at home with his parents. He was struggling in school, and they were coming down hard on him because of his grades. He had been placed on restriction for some time, and he thought it was unfair. I spoke with him several times and encouraged him to go home and talk it over with his dad. But three months later he was still being disciplined. It was then that I began to wonder whether he had ever spoken to his dad at all. When I confronted him, he said that he was afraid of his dad.

Because Jimmy feared his dad, he thought that if he ever said anything against his dad, if he ever disagreed with him, the consequences would be worse than the punishment for getting bad grades.

Does your child have the freedom to speak her mind in your home? Is there room for her to be open about her feelings, even if she disagrees with you? You may have a problem with this because you may think that if your child questions you in any way she is being disrespectful of you. Well, if this is the case, let me ask if you have spent time training her, bringing her up in the admonition of the Lord. If you have not, perhaps your child's problems or attitude are rooted in anger toward you. Colossians 3:21 tells us, "Fathers, do not provoke your children, lest they become discouraged"—spiritless, disheartened, or dismayed.

Dads can have a huge impact on their children—for good or for bad. It is naïve to think that your child's rebellion could not be related to her relationship with you. Again, this is not to blame you but to help you realize the awesome power you have in the life of your child. Satan wants you to think that you are not as influential as you are. He wants you to allow your kids to work it out on their own, because he knows that without a father's intervention—earthly and heavenly—he has a much better chance of accomplishing his goal: total destruction.

As a father, you don't have to be loud to be respected. You don't have to be mean to be followed. Again, your influence over your child will be empowered by your personhood.

While there is conflict in the home, keep Ephesians 4:29 in mind: "Let no corrupt word proceed out of your mouth, but what is good for necessary edification, that it may impart grace to the hearers." Ephesians 6:4 also offers good guidance: "And you, fathers, do not provoke your children to wrath, but bring them up in the training and admonition of the Lord." In other words, administer a mild rebuke or warning when possible, remembering that your responsibility is to raise your child to maturity.

The Bible says that it is in trials that we learn many valuable lessons for life. James 1:2–4: "My brethren, count it all joy when you fall into various trials, knowing that the testing of your faith produces patience. But let patience have its perfect work, that you may be perfect and complete, lacking nothing."

LIE #35: Quality time is better than quantity time.

For more than twenty years my parents attended the football games and boxing matches of their three sons. My brother and I played football from the age of ten to well into our twenties, and my other brother was a professional boxer. During that time lots of other dads commented on how obviously proud our dad was of his sons. We were good athletes, and as far as everyone else was concerned, we were good guys, too. (They didn't know about the trouble we got into.) We have always given our trophies and plaques to our dad, so his house is like a shrine.

Once a magazine writer came out to interview Dad about his boys. The million-dollar question was "What did you do to make all this happen with your sons?" His answer was simple, but perhaps a surprise: "I gave my sons my time. I tried to spend as much time with them as possible."

You have heard it said that the *quality* of time is better than the *quantity* of time. My friend, it requires a quantity of quality time to mold and shape character. It takes time to get to someone and transfer your values and principles for living to that person. It takes time to understand if you are giving quality time or not. There is no substitute for time together, doing anything and everything. Just look at your relationship with God. The Bible tells us to pray without ceasing, meaning that we need to spend all of our time in God's presence. He doesn't want just a few good minutes each day; he wants all of our day.

In the minds of busy dads, "quality" can sometimes mean setting a record for the shortest fishing trip on record or going to throw a football and counting the minutes until it is over, thinking you had a great time. Quality time with your child is not watching a clock but enjoying the time pass by with no end in sight. If your child is always preoccupied with when you are going to leave, she will never enjoy your time together.

With all of this said, what is a dad to do?

Review Questions

1. Are you as involved in your family as you are in your work?
2. Would you consider yourself a man of honor?
3. Do you enjoy spending time with your child?
4. Does your child's opinion mean anything to you?

Chemo-Prayers Time

Lie #29: The dad should depend on someone else, including the mom, to be the lead investigator in finding a cure for the wild child's cancer.

Dear Lord, I realize that you intend fathers to be priests in their homes. Even though mothers are intimately involved in the day-to-day running of the home, it is the father's responsibility to be most in touch with God, thus relaying God's message and power to the family. I pray for the strength to be that kind of a dad, a father who is in touch with all the issues in my child's life so that I can take them to you with intelligence and compassion.

[As a single mother, Lord, I pray that you would provide me with the wisdom, strength, and courage to assume this priestly role for the sake of my family.]

Lie #30: The dad is not responsible for his child's behavior.

Dear Lord, thank you for your Word. I thank you for making clear to me the high calling and responsibility that comes with being a father and the priest of my home. I pray for the strength to fulfill my priestly role with dignity and honor. Even though I realize that my child will suffer the consequences of his/her actions, I also realize that Proverbs 22:6 says, "Train up a child in the way he should go, And when he is old he will not depart from it." It is my responsibility to conduct this training, and I cannot do it without laying my life at your feet.

Lie #31: Moms and dads have the same influence on children.

Dear Lord, thank you for your love for me. I pray that you would help me as a father to realize that I have an entirely different role in my family from that of my wife. I pray that I would realize that as the body has many parts, I am a different part with a different influence and effect on my child. Please grant my wife and me the discernment to know how to maximize our roles and influence over our child. I know this influence is associated with different types of relationships. Please continue to make these differences clear.

Lie #32: A dad does not have to be a man of honor in order to be honored by his kids.

Dear Lord, thank you for your Word. How could I have ever thought that you would have called me to be the head of my wife and priest of the home while at the same time not being the most influential person in the family? Dear Lord, I acknowledge that in 1 Peter 1:16 you have called me to be holy, for you are holy.

Lie #33: You can be a good dad without being an involved dad.

Dear God, may I never believe this lie. In Mark 9 a dad whose son was demon possessed approached your Son for help. The father cried out, "But if You can do anything, have compassion on us and help us." I notice that in this father's plea he equated helping His son with helping him. This is simply because his son's problems were his problems. Please continue to show me that I need to be involved in my child's life.

Lie #34: A strong dad does not have to listen to the opinions of his kids. His opinion is the law.

Dear Lord, please remove this idea from my mind and heart. Matthew 5:5 says, "Blessed are the meek, for they shall inherit the earth." Meekness is defined as strength under control. The ultimate sign of strength is controlled strength. I know that as a father, the question I need to ask is not if I have power and strength but how well I use it for the good of my family. I know that I need to use my God-given strength to assume and not abuse my authority.

Lie #35: Quality time is better than quantity time.

Dear Lord, thank you for your Word. I realize that I must be more than the authoritarian in my home. I need to be the encourager, the listener, and the manager of everything going on in my home. First Timothy 5:8 says, "But if anyone does not provide for his own, and especially for those of his household, he has denied the faith and is worse than an unbeliever." Ephesians 6:4 says, "And you, fathers, do not provoke your children to wrath, but bring them up in the training and admonition of the Lord." God, I want to raise my child with love and encouragement as if you were here on earth raising him/her. Please don't give up on me as I pursue your calling on my life.

Afterword

IN MY FIRST PARENTING BOOK, *The Power of Believing in Your Child*, I challenged parents to believe that their children have been uniquely called by God to live a life far above the level of simply surviving. Jeremiah 29:11–12 says, "For I know the thoughts that I think toward you, says the Lord, thoughts of peace and not of evil, to give you a future and a hope." I believe this Scripture applies to all young people and that a miraculous turnaround can be made in order to secure the fulfillment of this verse in their lives.

I believe God has called all children to a life of great spiritual victory. Consequently, God has appropriately equipped them for such a life by giving them unlimited potential. My prayer was that after reading *The Power of Believing in Your Child*, when you looked at your children, you would begin to see signs of this potential. In other words, their physical, mental, emotional, social, and spiritual abilities would catch your eye sooner than their shortcomings. I then set out to encourage parents to begin treating their children differently by investing in this God-given potential.

My goal in writing *Parenting the Wild Child* was to encourage you to realize that the troubles your child is experiencing are the direct result of his or her engaging in, and possibly losing, a spiritual battle. This spiritual assault is based on well-designed lies presented in such a way so as to fool even the elect. These lies are aimed not only at your child but also at you. My desire was to expose the lies of the devil so that you could fight the unseen battle with spiritual night glasses.

> Finally, my brethren, be strong in the Lord and in the power of His might. Put on the whole armor of God, that you may be able to stand against the wiles of the devil. (Ephesians 6:10–11)

My prayer is that as you combat these issues on a spiritual level, God would begin to reveal to you the real issues behind the troubles and trials your child is facing. I pray that instead of living a life of defeat based on Satan's lies, you will begin to experience victory in Jesus based on the eternal truths of His Word. To help you do this, remember these three things:

TRUTH #1: God always has the last word.

"Heaven and earth will pass away, but My words will by no means pass away" (Mark 13:31).

No matter what Satan is telling you, God's Word will always be the most dependable source of guidance and counsel you can find.

TRUTH #2: Victory is already yours.

"You are of God, little children, and have overcome them, because He who is in you is greater than he who is in the world" (1 John 4:4).

No matter what is going on in the life of the wild child, Jesus is still DA MAN! No matter what you are going through, Jesus not only is fully aware of it but He is working through you to bring about a solution. And since He will always be King, the work that He is doing on your behalf will continue until the day of His return.

TRUTH #3: Obedience is the key.

"And we know that all things work together for good to those who love God, to those who are the called according to His purpose" (Romans 8:28).

Of the three truths presented here, this is the only one within your control. *All things working together for good* is up to God. And *being called* is up to God. But these good things only happen to those who love God and are called by Him. Only you can decide whether you love God and are called by Him. To show this, you obey Him. In all of your praying, disciplining, communicating, and fighting the battle before you, the number one thing you must do is obey God throughout the process.

I hope you have been encouraged to begin fighting the good fight. Remember that you are fighting this battle from a position of victory, not one in pursuit of victory.

———

Throughout this book you have gotten to know Caroline. On March 31, 2000, she lost her battle with breast cancer but won her game of life. I would like to thank her not only for her contribution to this book but also for being a role model to me. She was truly a woman of God and has left a strong legacy of spiritual integrity and faithfulness. She is survived by her husband, Brad, and four daughters.

APPENDIX A

LIES AIMED AT PARENTS

LIE #1: The wild child is the enemy.

LIE #2: You have the right to demand a child to stop his or her wildness before you understand the wildness.

LIE #3: The wild child has no reason for his or her wildness.

LIE #4: You have a right not to allow the problems of your wild child to interfere with your life.

LIE #5: The wild child truly understands and fears the consequences of his or her actions.

LIE #6: Satan is not involved in the details of your life.

LIE #7: The bad timing of the wild child's troubles is only a coincidence.

LIE #8: All of your troubles are God's fault.

LIE #9: Your child will never change.

LIE #10: The situation surrounding the wild child will never change.

LIE #11: You are a failure as a parent.

LIE #12: Prayers are just as effective whether they are organized or not.

LIE #13: Praying for others won't work unless they have a desire to change.

LIE #14: If my wild child's behavior is not improving, my prayers must not be working.

LIE #15: All I need to do is pray, and everything will work out for good.

LIE #16: God knows my needs; therefore, I don't need to pray about specific details.

LIE #17: Rules in the home will take the fun out of your relationship with your child.

LIE #18: Parents don't have a right to know and control everything that happens in the home.

LIE #19: Your child deserves a hangout of his or her own that is off limits to parents.

LIE #20: Children know right from wrong and don't need discipline.

LIE #21: If I start disciplining my child, he will rebel even more and I will lose him.

LIE #22: A little dose of discipline now and then will be

enough to straighten out a wild child.

LIE #23: If my child makes me mad, he deserves whatever trouble comes his way.

LIE #24: Talking *to* the wild child is the same as communicating *with* the wild child.

LIE #25: Even though my child and I don't talk much, we still have a strong relationship.

LIE #26: It's unnecessary to talk to my child about important issues because she shares my same beliefs.

LIE #27: Since I cannot sustain a long conversation with my child, there must be a problem.

LIE #28: If I see things from my child's perspective, it will encourage more wild behavior.

LIE #29: The dad should depend on someone else, including the mom, to be the lead investigator in finding a cure for the wild child's cancer.

LIE #30: The dad is not responsible for his child's behavior.

LIE #31: Moms and dads have the same influence on children.

LIE #32: A dad does not have to be a man of honor in order to be honored by his kids.

LIE #33: You can be a good dad without being an involved dad.

LIE #34: A strong dad does not have to listen to the opinion of his kids. His opinion is the law.

LIE #35: Quality time is better than quantity time.

APPENDIX B

LIES AIMED AT THE WILD CHILD

LIE #1: God is not going to take care of your needs.

LIE #2: Your life will always be filled with pain; therefore, embrace it.

LIE #3: The benefits of meeting your own needs outweigh the consequences.

LIE #4: Why use your strengths for godly purposes when they can be used to meet your own needs?

LIE #5: There's no need to resist temptations.

LIE #6: If you don't take control of your life, you are a chump.